Boathouse Boy

YOUNG SUMMERS ON AMERICAN LAKE

Boathouse Boy

YOUNG SUMMERS ON AMERICAN LAKE

BY

LOUIS M. RAPHAEL

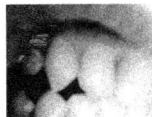

CANTANKEPRESS

Dedication

To my family:

Gidget and Phil, Jeff and Sierra, Wes and Lindsey, Carol,

Chelsea, Alexis and Bryan.

Thanks for making me feel like one of you.

Special thanks to Weston, my grandson and "publisher."

Louis M. Raphael

Contents

Preface

A few days before Christmas, 1941, a rough-hewn big man of German heritage visited the Tacoma, Wash., home of one of his daughters, Ruth, nee Seidelman. Grandpa Seidelman was old enough to retire, but he was single and did not own a home of his own. So he continued to work and had accepted a job running a boathouse on American Lake, south of Tacoma.

The Japanese had just attacked Pearl Harbor and the nation was in full mobilization. Virtually all able-bodied men and many women rushed to join the armed forces or to work for industries building ships and planes and tanks.

John Seidelman needed a little bit of help at the boathouse so that he could get occasional rest and could get to town once a week to visit relatives and make a few purchases. He eyed the "labor pool" available and decided to enlist his 14-year-old grandson, Ruth's son Louis, as part-time help.

So he made an offer to the boy after consulting with Ruth: $40 per month and room and board, from June through August. It was an offer too good to turn down and the boy was delighted. In truth, he would have accepted the job without the salary. Louis performed the duties of boathouse boy for two years until he became old enough at age 16 to work in the shipyards.

No one could have predicted how important those days at the lake would prove to the boy. It was a case of lifelong love that proved to be a significant factor in his lengthy life.

Louis with brothers Jack and Billy Paul.

— The Girl on the Diving Board —

Sometimes things happen to us that may or may not seem important at the time. But much later in the wisdom of our mellowing, we look back and see them in a different light.

It was that way with me when I was age 14 and one day became privileged to see my first naked female breast.

The breast in question, and another identical to it, belonged to the teenage girl next door, who happened to be sunning on the diving board of the lakeside cottage at American Lake her family had rented for the summer.

She was stretched out prone, sleepily enjoying the moderate sun and lack of wind on an early summer day when I just happened – honest – to be a few feet below and to the west of her in a rowboat on one of my many rowing and fishing expeditions the summer I first worked for Grandfather at the boathouse. It was a one-in-millions happening. As Rick said in "Casablanca," of all the diving boards on the lake, of all the lakes in the county, she had to . . . .

The young woman was probably 16 or 17 years old, brunette, comely, and lithe. Her little brother had been over to the boathouse and had gone fishing with me a time or two. Her father had taken young Billy and me for a speedboat run in a ChrisCraft one day. It was one of very few powerboats on the lake in that time of gas rationing. My rowboat was much more the norm. All the boats we had at the boathouse were powered by oars. We did not have even one outboard motor to rent.

Anyway, this young woman was pretty, but the sight of a special area of her skin did not excite me at all. I was just becoming aware of girls and noting that they were, perhaps, more than just a silly bunch of gigglers who were useless at sports and had better stay on their own side of the playground, where a couple of sissies had joined them to swing and play with dolls.

Indeed, my friend Jim and I were flat-out ignorant of the anatomical features of women, young and old. We knew that they were different, because they wore different clothes, especially those things on their chests. But we puzzled a lot about what might lie beneath those shielding cloth blinders.

Inside the shack on the boathouse dock where I slept by myself or with Jim snoozing away across the room on my "guest" cot, there was an enameled sheetmetal advertisement for Coca Cola. It featured a sexy girl in a two-piece bathing suit. Jim and I often stared at that girl, but we were ignorant of what her body might look like in the flesh.

The sunbather gave me my chance to solve half our questions. I had perhaps half a second to look and remember as the young woman suddenly reared up, perhaps in response to a squeak of my oars. She just as rapidly flopped back down.

There are many images burned on my mind, but not this one. I can see the diving board and the shoreline, the gold of sun on the water, and our nearby dock. But I have to reconstruct the girl and her bathing suit – I am sure it was dark, and obviously two-piece because she had undone the straps on her back so as to get an even tan.

Rather than an erotic image – you must remember that I didn't know what the hell erotic was – I had a sense of appreciation. Boy, that was beautiful!

I still feel that way today. Yes, breasts have become erotic to me, now that I have thought about it, but I have never joined those who snicker and titter – yes, on purpose – about the upper portion of the female anatomy.

Once I knew a young woman, briefly, who would not let a lover – and she had several, at least – see her topside naked. "I am so big," she said. Many men I know would go crazy at the thought.

Not I. Moderation in all things – right? A variation in size is no turnoff. We are endowed by our Creator . . . .

I worked with a woman once in my penultimate part-time job who was so huge upstairs that she had to have surgical reduction. She was a 300 pounder, as was her sister, and they both bent over when they walked. Pity.

Another woman I knew had one breast removed and reconstructed. She looked and felt fine. Her life went on 100 percent.

One time in the newsroom at the paper, a group of men and women were having a discussion. Terminology for mammaries came up. I agreed wholeheartedly with the arts editor who said she did not like the term boobies "because it sounded like it was a mistake."

Back to the girl on the diving board. She went to Catholic schools and her family was Irish. Her brother apparently felt that I was attracted to her, because he said to me, "You are too young for her." I agreed.

It happened that I saw the girl about four years later when I was in the Army at Fort Lewis. She was in the PX with two or three handsome blond fellows who seemed to be a bit girlish.

I did not know what a homosexual was in those days, but some GIs who were getting doughnuts and coffee at the same time made some remarks about the young men and the girl. I only half understood.

That the girl on the diving board turned out to prefer women or girls to men or boys did not diminish my happy memory of that day when I first realized that there was indeed something delightful about females that I could appreciate, along with other qualities.

And there are some qualities I do not appreciate. But that is another story.

You heard it here first.

— A Day at the Boathouse —

Grandpa Seidelman stood in the sunshine outside the front and only door to his green plywood shack. The old Bavarian chewed with his usual contentment on a cheap stogie and looked out with pleasure on the scene before him: placid American Lake with its cold, deep waters and the forested shores of Silcox Island looming a half mile away. Further across the lake stood the cream-colored buildings of the Veterans' Hospital. To his left and right, the shoreline bellied out to a pair of points. In between these points, cottages and larger homes took up all the shoreline. Some of them had boathouses and almost every one had at least a modest dock or anchored float.

The old man had reason to feel good. Almost all of the 57 boats from Don's Boathouse had been rented already this Sunday mid-morn. The going rate was twenty-five cents per hour or seventy-five for a day's rent of an ordinary rowboat. One larger boat went for a dollar, and it was the one the Swedes packed their family into so they could catch more fish on an outing. There were three round-bottomed boats for trollers tied to the dock.

Many boats were rented by soldiers from nearby Fort Lewis, especially on weekends. The Army base was swollen with troops during World War II, and the GIs took advantage of their time off to go to nearby Tacoma or Olympia for recreation. A number of them had discovered the beautiful lake where they could rent a boat and forget their duties and concerns for a few hours. Not a few had brought along a few beers. Some of them even had fishing tackle, but they generally arrived at the boathouse too late for the good early morning fishing, so they took it easy in the sun and light breeze and enjoyed life.

Grandpa's shack served both as domicile and office. The front six feet or so inside the door was the office. It had a small window facing on the lake to the west and a primitive sort of desk or shelf under the window. One could look out the window while renting a boat and say, "Take No. 17 there," pointing generally to a sturdy rowboat alongside others, all painted green and with white numbers on the bows. As boatboy, it was my duty to carry seat cushions and oars out to the designated boat and push the occupants out into the water after they had put their gear inside and seated themselves.

When there were no more boats to rent, the business day was not finished – far from it. As those who had rented by the hour or had satisfied their desire for waterborne recreation for the day came in, I helped them by pulling their boat up on the sandy shore and making sure things were shipshape for the next customer. Sometimes the same boat would be rented out three or more times on a busy Sunday.

Mr. Don Gawley would be pleased, Grandpa thought. He was an easy going sort, anyway, and he trusted Grandpa to make an honest accounting. Mr. Gawley and his wife lived a short distance up the hill on the boathouse property in one of two houses thereon. They and their renters worked at Fort Lewis or the Mt. Rainier Ordnance Depot, which everyone called the motor base. The boathouse was a source, and a good one, of supplemental income for the Gawleys.

Grandpa threw his cigar stub left-handed well up on the hill toward the big fir tree and turned to clamber up into his office/dormitory. One was reminded, seeing the old man wind up, that most bears are supposed to be left-pawed. There was at least a slight resemblance.

Inside the shack, a radio was playing. Grandpa turned it up. He moved into the other part of the building. There was a thin plywood wall between the two parts. In the inner part, there was a bed and a straight chair and a small table to one side and a wood stove on the other. Under that bed he had a bottle of schnapps. The only time anyone ever knew of his drinking anything alcoholic was first thing in the morning when he reached down and got the bottle and swallowed his "eye-opener."

On the wood stove, Grandpa cooked three meals a day except on his day off, when he went to town and left the place in my charge. One might wonder at this, but there was no apparent alternative, and Gramps trusted me even though I was only fourteen. He shared his meals 50-50 with me. He always seemed to be patient, even when I did not readily respond to his call to quit fishing and settle down at the breakfast table with him. Sometimes he would have to go out over the plank gangway to the large dock to see if I was sleeping late, which rarely if ever happened. He would spot me, anchored about fifty yards out in the lake where the springs are.

He would shout out to me to come in for breakfast, and I would hear him unless the fish were biting especially well.

On this particular summer day there were a few swimmers. Part of the old building on the dock consisted of a couple of booths or small rooms where an occasional swimmer could change clothes. A giddy girl swimming with two high school boys sang out, "No fair peeking now." All three giggled.

Grandpa was looking for something as he entered his inner sanctum. He slept in a single twin bed in the corner. We may never know what it was he sought, because he couldn't find it. He likely forgot what he was seeking, because Grandpa was no longer young, and his memories were selective, but entertaining.

He would tell, for example about the time when he was fishing in Wisconsin, where he worked at a mill, and the angling was especially bleak. "Throw it in again, John, I said," he said. "And damned if I didn't snag a 26-pound muskellunge." Or the time a large trout in a stream in Idaho took several baits off his hook. Grandpa dried some salmon eggs in the sun on his hook and prepared to cast. "All right, Mr. Cocky," he said, after assuring the listener that the fish could have "hit those eggs till hell froze over and not get them off." Anyway, he caught the fish.

He wandered back out to the office and took a seat at the stool in front of the desk. Two more boats had returned to the boathouse and he made a check beside the 75¢ on the line he filled out to register each rental. That meant the boat was in okay and was eligible to rent out again. On the rest of the line were signature, boat number, time out and in. A renter had to sign his name.

Soon it was almost noon and time to cook something for himself and one perpetually hungry boy. Fairly often, I brought in fresh-caught fish for the old man to cook. Whether he made flapjacks or cooked spuds and onions and porkchops, John divided everything, sometimes it seemed dangerously, with a chef's knife: right up the middle: fair and square. Now just as he was thinking to move toward the stove again with culinary intent, he became aware that someone was leisurely walking down the hill toward the office. It was a soldier: an officer, and he had a gentle smile and hummed to himself as he approached.

Grandpa moved the few steps to the doorway in anticipation of a probable boat rental. He had turned up the radio but was not listening intently as "The Hour of Prayer" blared away. A fish flopped in the outer portion of the short channel of water that cut between the two docks of the boathouse. Chubby and Butch, a cocker and a pit bull belonging to the Gawleys, came racing down the hill past the officer. Butch leaped out onto the smaller dock and just about had a fit barking at a pair of mallards swimming close by.

The officer approached. Grandpa was ready to rent another boat before lunch. He was about to pick up the pencil beside the book when the soldier said, "I see you listen to The Hour of Power."

Grandpa had long been naturalized. But, basically, he was just a hard-working German immigrant with no formal education. He did not notice the officer had little gold crosses on his uniform along with the oakleaves of a major. Nor did he know that the crosses designated a chaplain.

"Oh, yes," Grandpa smiled, taking a freshly lit cigar out of the corner of his mouth for a few seconds. "I like to listen to them fellows bullshit."

— A List-topping Lake —

It was our family's good fortune that, when the Great Depression and the miserable climate of Missouri forced a move to greener pastures, we landed in Tacoma.

It could have been Seattle or Everett or Portland, Oregon. It could have been anywhere in the country where we had relatives who could extend a helping hand and let us lean on them for support.

As it turned out, my maternal grandmother's second husband, George Reid, was a longshoreman with steady employment out of the union hall in downtown Tacoma. George and Sophie had a mortgage of about $3,000 on a nice old house on M Street, about half the way to South Tacoma and up the hill from downtown and the busy port where George labored on the docks, loading and unloading seagoing vessels. The waterfront in those days had just a few remaining sawmills of the 31 it was said existed on Commencement Bay some years earlier when Tacoma billed itself as "The Lumber Capital of the World."

Grandfather Reid worked mainly if not exclusively at the Baker Dock. I think it is still there after all these years. Nearby was the Sperry Mills facility, where ships loaded up cargoes of flour. One large sawmill remaining was that of St. Paul & Tacoma Lumber Co., which later became Simpson. I do not know when the pulp mills began to flourish, but their pungent smell reached back to my childhood days.

From Green to Green

Grandfather Reid was Grandmother's second husband. We children always accepted him as if he had been our biological relative. In those days, divorce was a somewhat scandalous matter, and we never talked about it or even thought of it for that matter.

George Reid had been born in Ireland. He sailed around the Horn of South America as a youth on a sailing vessel in that day when the masts of those graceful and silent ships made a kind of forest of their own in Tacoma's harbor.

His journey from Ireland landed him eventually in the Evergreen State's second city. As a sailor and then a stevedore, he was never far from the smell of saltwater.

Somewhere in his career, he had worked in logging camps, I believe as a cook. He had also worked on a railroad in Central America, probably after the ship's captain put the troublesome young Irishman ashore.

George could drink beer with the best of them and he gambled, usually at craps. He frequented the Brittania Tavern and the Swiss Hall in downtown Tacoma on the way home with his longshore co-workers, Hank and Doggie and others. Several times, he claimed, he came within one natural throw of the dice to having won enough to retire the mortgage on the family home. Occasionally his friends would dump him, drunk as a lord, on Grandma's front porch. His tie and perhaps his suspenders would be cut in two and he would roll his eyes and cry out "Never again, Mama," to a disgusted Sophia, who had been there before.

Speaking of that property, it included a small but adequate house on the alley behind Grandma's house or the "big house." Six of us in our family at one time lived in the small house, and my Uncle Bill and Aunt Lois had lived there for a while early in their marriage before our residency.

We were cramped in our little house, but we survived well and the children in our family did very well academically and athletically at school. We ate wonderfully well and were adequately clothed.

A Move up Front

After our obese and sickly grandmother died, Mother and the three kids remaining at home moved into the big house and Grandpa Reid happily moved to the smaller house behind. My older brother Jack had graduated from high school in 1941 and he joined the RCAF when he could not get into the U.S. Army Air Force because he was too young. Soon he was flying Hurricanes and Spitfires in England and, by default, I became the man of the house. Mother did George's housekeeping and made sure he had good food until his last days.

The only lake I recalled having seen up to age 14 was Wapato Lake, a muddy swamplike body not far south of us. The neighborhood kids sometimes went there to swim in the summer and risked their lives during some winters when ice formed just thick enough to support forms of play such as "hockey" with a tin can and no ice skates.

So it was a revelation when I first saw American Lake. I did not know what to expect but readily accepted everything about the lake and the boathouse and all that went with life at the Gawleys' place. The room in the shack was more than adequate, and the meals cooked up by Grandpa always hit the spot.

From our viewpoint on the east shore, we looked across to the wooded large island and beyond to The Vets' Hospital on the western shore. To the south of the hospital was the wooded expanse of Fort Lewis property. Toward the north were private homes and a boathouse that later became a park.

On the eastern side of the lake, points of land both north and south gave way gently to our location. Homes both small and obviously meant for vacation occupancy sat side by side with fancier digs. To the far north were the luxurious facilities of a country club and a fancy golf course. There were no unoccupied waterfront properties apparent.

It was a mixture of civilization and the wild that seemed to provide something for everyone. That, to me, is American Lake in essence: everything one would want in a lake.

I have fished a number of lakes in Pierce and other counties: Spanaway, Gravelly, St. Clair, Hicks, Summit, Lawrence – the list goes on and on. But I have to put American Lake at the top of the heap overall of all the lowland lakes I have known.

Long, Wide, Deep

The lake itself had to be a gift of the Ice Age that once gripped this land. A beautiful neighboring lake, Gravelly, must have been born at the same time. Both lakes are deep – American deeper – and are spring fed, although Gravelly lacks the stream inlet that Murray Creek provides to American.

The ice sheet that once covered our area also left a number of big boulders here and there across the landscape. One of these was on the vacant lot across from the fire station where we used to play ball and dig trenches and where Jerry Hartman broke his leg by tripping on a berry vine as he ran the bases. Others were scattered around our end of town. There is a doozy near the freeway at 56th St. and Tacoma Mall Blvd.

American Lake is located eight miles southwest of Tacoma. It is three and a half miles long, including the large area known as Little American Lake, and about a mile wide at the widest. The depth plummets to 90 feet in spots to the west and north of Silcox, the large wooded island that dominates the center of the lake.

There are five islands: Silcox, and its smaller companions, Short, Barlow, Cors, and Beard and one location that I often refer to as "the sunken island." This latter spot is west of the point with a sign warning of military control to the south. A goodly distance from shore it is shallow and weedy. Trollers would do well to know where it is.

A large underwater bar runs roughly east and west between the officers' beach facility and the National Guard's Camp Murray.

Some areas such as the stretch between two of the small islands and Little American Lake are among the shallower parts. The little lake at the extreme south end is connected with the much larger lake proper by a shallow and narrow waterway.

Little American Lake is little only by comparison with the larger lake. It is larger than several lakes I have fished in Pierce and Thurston counties and in the Cascade foothills.

The little lake has a depth of 40 feet at the maximum. All the land around it is military controlled and most all of it is forested. Housing for military families sits atop a hill on the west side and a non-commissioned officers' club building sits back far enough from the east side that one may ignore it if so desired.

An underwater plateau of sorts – is there such a thing? – takes up an area that seems football-field in size on the north side of Silcox Island. I learned about this plateau by trial and error when I was growing up and fishing the lake whenever possible. Now, with the advent of the electronic depth finder, any dub can readily see what I sweated to learn. A fisherman with a depth finder and an electric trolling motor has a great edge on the fish.

The waters of the lake have always appeared remarkably clear. We did not hesitate to drink directly out of the lake when I was living there. After all, there were only a handful of gasoline-powered motors on the entire lake. So we washed our dishes and ourselves right at the lakeshore by our living quarters. I combined abortive efforts to teach myself to swim with what passed for my baths. The water was too cold for me. The muscles I had were fine for playing baseball and football, but I never got the hang of swimming. Even today, water is good for two things in my life: fishing and making ice cubes for highballs.

I can attest that sand makes a good abrasive for both plates and skin, although it can be a bit rough on hands.

Hark, Hark, the Carp

In the old days it seemed the lake was virtually weed free, or at least it had many fewer weeds. It has been said that the carp ate the weeds, and I cannot deny it. Anyway, since the big poisoning with rotenone, vegetation has flourished. The carp are long gone. I don't know all the biological implications of this, but you can hook into more weeds these days than before without hardly trying.

I Christen Thee

At the southern end of the little lake, there is another lake. It is not connected to American Lake and a road runs between the two bodies of water. But Sequallitchew Lake is so close to American that I was tempted to fish in it. I only had to beach my boat and hike a short distance to do this. However, anyone I talked to discouraged me. They said Sequallitchew was shallow, and a reference book says it is 17 feet deep. Besides, said those advising me, there are only spiny rays there and American has much better fishing. I happily took this advice.

When I was in the Army in 1946, a sergeant I knew slightly did catch a medium-sized bass from the shore.

But Sequallitchew turns out to be important historically. A military expedition led by Gen. Wilkes spent Independence Day there back in the 1800s and it was then they named American Lake for the patriotic occasion.

Tiny Tillicum

The little settlement of Tillicum sits on the eastern flank of American Lake. It has historically been the home to military families in the main. Jim and I were amused one time while on one of our walking expeditions to see signs on lawns and fences: Sgt. Johnson, Capt. Lewis, Private Road – oops.

So far as I know, Tillicum has never been incorporated. I do not believe it has a mayor or council or town hall or any of that. But it does have The Barbecue Inn, which was an old place when I first saw it and which still stands today. There is a Galloping Gertie Room in the inn, named after the first Narrows Bridge that fell down in high winds in 1940. I never saw the inside of the eatery and likely never will.

There may be a small church or two in Tillicum, but I can't say for sure. Pretty much just residences, most of them small and needing a facelift. There are some modest newer apartments. The insurance building Jim Hutson came to own when his insurance business flourished is one of the larger ones in town – two stories.

The Competition

I guess you can say Firch's Boathouse was in Tillicum, although it is hard for me to think of waterfront property as part of the village. Firch's old location is now part of Harry Todd Park. The boat rental business is history and Mr. Firch's stentorian voice as he chews out someone throwing rocks at ducks must still be echoing someplace nearby.

The boathouse catered somewhat to swimmers. When I was a young teacher, my wife and I took our little son, less than two years old, swimming there. I had an experience that made me think of the girl on the diving board.

It seems some enterprising lady, maybe as old as 30, had made herself a bathing suit. Only she used jersey and that turned out to be a no-no because when she came out of the water, it was obvious to one and all that a goodly part of her suit had been ingested, so to speak, by her body. She remedied this quickly, but the anatomy lesson, though brief, was clear.

I reflected that had I seen the lady emerging when I was the boy at the boathouse, I would have been years ahead in my perception of the feminine body. However, I gladly settled for the top half of my earlier experience, as if I had a choice.

Today there is a shell house right next to or possibly in the park where the rowers store their graceful sculls between outings. This structure looms large from out on the lake. It looks a little like an airplane hangar, and I used it as a triangulation point when trolling north of the island on clearer days.

Just a little north of the park is Thornewood, that large old red brick structure. It has been in several movies and has a long history of its own. It was named after Chester Thorne, the original builder and owner.

But aside from a brief period in later years when I paid a nominal monthly rental to keep my homemade rowboat at Firch's, and a few family swimming outings at the park, the area near Firch's was alien territory for me. Jim and I seldom wandered that way. We kept almost entirely to the south in our outings and away from what Grandpa referred to as "Kerch's." But then, the old German also called a church a "kerch" and milk was "milch."

Milk, milch, Firch, Kerch – who cares? What is important is that they're getting a few. That was a pat answer Grandfather gave to just about any inquiry from a fisherman. Its truth smooths out a large array of petty differences.

Grandpa George Reid and Grandma Sophia Knabe Reid in front of the house at 4105 South M Street.

— My Home in Tacoma —

My delight at living and working at American Lake was not predicated on pleasure at getting away from home. Although our family's economic means were severely limited, my three siblings and I led enjoyable lives.

We always had ample and tasty food. Mother was a good cook, although the old wood stove could have been better and easier to use. She also baked great cakes and rolls and bread, although her pies sometimes had undercooked lower crusts.

I didn't care. I appreciated the quality and I ate with gusto. No sweet potato or doughnut dare show itself to me without danger of being devoured. And Mom encouraged what developed into gluttony, I am afraid. It is a wonder I do not weigh 300 pounds because I ate huge amounts. Only my extremely active lifestyle prevented obesity. I ran everywhere. My friends on bikes going to another neighborhood for a ballgame or arrow fight would find me easily keeping up next to them, giving my Keds a good workout.

Location, Location, Etc.

The property at 4105 So. M St. was superbly located for most purposes. We were next to the corner of M and 41st and our neighbor was a vacant lot. Across M Street from us were a small grocery store, a butcher shop, a car repair service, and a small candy company's factory and retail outlet. M Street was an arterial, but there were few cars and trucks putting by. When we first moved to Tacoma, the street car line ran between downtown and South Tacoma, but the rails were taken up shortly before World War II and buses took the place of street cars.

The church we attended was up the block on the opposite corner from us, diagonally across from the red brick fire station. We attended Sunday School there, not that it did much for my immortal soul. The preacher's redheaded son, Eddie Goodnough, was a friend and playmate until the Methodist Church transferred the dad to Seattle.

In the opposite direction, a block away, was our elementary school, Whitman. It was built in the 1880's and our mother had graduated from eighth grade there. My siblings and I all attended this fine old school, as did all of my ball-playing buddies. Best of all, there was a sandy baseball field next to the school where most of the boys in our neighborhood spent many happy hours playing baseball and other sports. There were two basketball hoops with rims about six feet in height and soccer goal posts that we used for dropkicking field goals during our touch football games.

The boys who made up the heart of our neighborhood teams lived nearby. Four of my closest friends were clustered around the intersection of 41st and L St., a short block away from our home via the alley that bisected our block. Our activities centered around that intersection when we were not at the school playfield.

Ah, Wilderness!

In those days there were a number of vacant lots with trees and brush, including wild berries and nuts. Kids roamed all around the neighborhood, playing ball games on L Street and cops and robbers and other games in vacant lots and yards of tolerant residents. Dogs were free to roam everywhere and few were licensed.

Up M Street a block to the south, there was a small convenience store where Harold Hauge sold candy and bread and redeemed empty beer bottles for a few pennies. Some kids from the neighborhood also sat on the few stools there and bought shakes and pop to consume on the premises.

Three movie theaters were about equidistant from our home. The Capitol, Community, and Rex were all patronized by us kids. We paid a dime or eleven cents for admission to the double features.

Kids under six were let in free, and most of us lied about the ages of our younger siblings.

Further away but in easy walking distance to us was Lincoln High School. It stood next to a baseball field with lights and all the trappings necessary for the Tacoma City League games. We attended games regularly and tried to find home run balls hit over the fences and down into the Lincoln Gulch. When no games were being played, we often played on the sandy field ourselves.

To the west of us and down the hill a bit was a large undeveloped area that later became the Tacoma Mall and all the other commercial entities that sprung up there after the war.

As you can surmise, our childhoods were not ones of deprivation.

All that changed somewhat when World War II burst upon the scene. By then I was a veteran of the 22-block walk to J. P. Stewart Intermediate School, where almost all the kids from Whitman went.

We felt privileged to live within sound of our grade school bell, a block away from our church, and on the busline. It was a happy situation, and my summers of playing ball, drinking home made rootbeer, taking part in weeklong games of Monopoly, and hiking to the wooded areas and the grasslands where the freeway would one day be located were happy days well wasted.

The Luckiest Boy

But when Grandfather beckoned me to come to American Lake and to open a new chapter in my young life, I leaped at the chance.

One of our neighborhood boys had a dad who worked for the railroad and who arranged for him to travel to Wisconsin a summer or two for a month-long stay with grandparents. We missed our buddy and were glad to have him back, but I did not envy him.

Now I was the one to have an exotic opportunity, and I was not about to miss it.

I had not felt like an outsider when several of us hiked out to Wapato Lake in the summer. Other boys swam, but I stayed out of the water. I did not try to swim until years later in high school when that activity was a requirement. Besides, my mother was just as glad. It was widely thought that polio was contracted by swimming in lakes like Wapato, which was not much better than a mudhole. The coldness of the water at American Lake prevented me from learning to swim during my time there.

Again, I was about the only one in my age range in our group that did not have a bike, nor skates for that matter, until a generous little girl who lived up by the firehall gave me a spare pair. This not only did not hold me down, but I never even thought of being envious.

So now I more or less accepted my good fortune in stride. I had no idea how wonderful life at the lake would be, but I was determined to go ahead regardless. The sandlot baseball games at Whitman would have to do without me for a while.

— Shorty, Larry, and the Tackle Box —

During my pleasant employment at the boathouse, there were a number of visitors, some of them regulars. They did not come to see me, but they accepted me as a part of reality. Almost all of them came to visit Grandfather, who was known as "Dad" or "Dad Seidelman" to most of them.

Paramount among the trickle of humanity were two persons: Larry Feir and Shorty. I never knew Shorty's name, either first or last, but I remember him well.

As for Larry, he was a kid with a short blond haircut and glasses. He was a student at Clover Park High School, which was only a few years old at the time, if not brand new.

Larry didn't say much, but with me around he didn't get much opportunity, I suspect. At the time, I was fixated upon being a sports hero. In order to do this, I had to play football at a high school level. And, in order to play, one had to have football shoes with round, hard cleats and soft kangaroo skin uppers.

It was during my second year with Gramps that the shoes began to grow in importance as I neared entering high school, so I talked more and more about them. Larry noted this and commented, not unkindly, about my fixation.

Since Larry didn't say much, I can't tell you what he said. But he did come regularly to spend time in and out of the small area where we collected rentals and kept the books. I guess you could say he just hung around for whatever scraps of conversation he could hear.

It seems ironic to me now that Larry did play football at Clover Park, while my football "career" at Lincoln High was quite limited after I proved to myself that I was too small and/or not dedicated enough to endure sawdust in the jockstrap and sore muscles from poundings from bigger boys.

That I should even mention Larry points out the paucity of regular visitors we had. Most of the time it was just Gramps and me, or one of us and the dogs. I had plenty of time for fishing and introspection, both of which were indulged in to the fullest.

I guess my friend Jim Hutson would have to be the third most frequent visitor, but Jim was more like my alter ego rather than a visitor, so I will talk about him elsewhere.

Short a Little Bit

Shorty was just that. I am sure that I was every bit as tall as he, which was not very. He had a hump on one side of his back and/or shoulder that bulged out from his clothing like he was carrying a small ham home for dinner. The hump seemed to make him list to one side a little, but we all pretended that it was not there, and our conversations with Shorty were pleasant. But come to think of it, I don't think he smiled much.

At the time, the war effort had sucked up almost all of the male population and some of the women, too. Rosie the Riveter was on everyone's mind. My Aunt Ruth worked for a while at a Boeing Co. sub-assembly facility in South Tacoma. Of course, virtually all the able-bodied guys were in the armed forces. The remaining ones were involved in essential work of one kind or another.

Then there were the 4-Fs. These were men with physical or mental problems that kept them out of the Army or Navy. I am sure Shorty was one of them. The Selective Service took one look at his hump, never mind his stature, and he was disqualified.

Being 4-F did not prevent a man from working in the shipyards or at Boeing, if he could perform the duties of the job. In fact, many older guys – there were also age restrictions for military duty – worked two full shifts a day. I taught school after the war with a married couple who both worked fulltime as teachers and then another eight hours a day in the shipyards. Many a family built a nest egg in this way while most of the male population was off fighting the Japanese or Germans.

At any rate, there was Shorty. I don't know what he did most of the time nor what employment he might have held, but he was good enough company around the boathouse.

He seemed to tend to think a lot and to speak freely enough. And I learned a thing or two from him about fishing.

The main thing I learned was how to make a worm sandwich and the prerequisite step, which was to cover the hook, eye and all, with bait. This was supposed to avoid spooking the fish by showing the metal glint of the hook.

Shorty illustrated how to bait the hook by actually doing it for me one day when he came to fish off the dock and to converse with Dad or "Pops" Seidelman.

He took half an angle worm and threaded it onto a number nine or ten hook on a leader. "Then run the bait up the leader past the hook," he said as he did just that. Then he worked the wriggling worm segment back to cover all but the sharp tip of the hook.

Shorty took an orange salmon egg from a bait jar and carefully speared it on the hook end. It made the perfect ambush for an innocent perch or trout. Not a modicum of metal showed through.

Shorty came as close to smiling as I ever remember. He was making his contribution to society.

A Box of Treasures

Gramps was paying me well enough. The $40 a month was more than adequate for a job that I would have gladly done for free. But there were other perks to my employment. I have already mentioned the liberal opportunities to fish. My bed and food were satisfactory in every way, and the old man was wise enough to treat me very well in word as well as in deed.

An unexpected bonus came in the form of an old fishing box that held bits and pieces of tackle. Doubtless these had been thrown into the box when forgetful fishermen had left them behind. Old Man Dittemore, the owner who sold the boathouse to Gawley, possibly felt someone would come back for a favorite piece of tackle, so he held on to leftovers for a number of years.

I sorted through this box with Gramps' approval and clipped hooks off pieces of leader, salvaged leaden shot from the same source, and delighted in the three or four plugs and one star-drag reel that popped up.

The plugs included a big green crayfish that swam backwards, a corroded River Runt Spook, a plug with red head and white body, and a treble hook and spinner with big yellow and red feathers. These were all large lures with formidable hooks. I don't recall fishing with any of them, because as soon as I could afford small Helin Flatfish, these were what I used to catch fish trolling. But the old lures are still around somewhere in my own collection of snagged leaders, rusty hooks, bobbers, and the like that are stored in my basement.

The one item that was really a find defied my putting it to good use. Oh, I did fish with it a few times but never figured out how to use it properly. And my lack of understanding cost me a chance at the most sizeable trout I had hooked up to that time. But I will tell you about that later. Suffice it to say that it was a star-drag reel and I did not understand how it worked. If I had, it could have helped advance my career as an angler.

I was always loath to ask anyone too many questions. I almost flunked geometry in high school because I tried to figure out those thorny problems alone rather than ask help from our witch-like teacher. This is strange, because I have no compunction about hopping out of the car to ask directions at any gas station or home, for that matter.

Don't Ask, Don't Learn

Ironically, in later years when I finally learned to catch kokanee at the lake by trolling, I employed a wonderful star-drag reel to do the trick. It took me until my late 60's or 70's at least to reach the goal.

Today, I am too feeble to fish for the "silvers," but I can tell you how to catch them trolling. Maybe I will.

In the meantime, I'll live with the memories and the esoteric knowledge. Fishermen are a varied lot. Most of them have their own methods and favorite lures or baits. Or they are still trying to figure it out for themselves.

For my own part, I picked up a little hint here and there and slowly put it all together until I could be satisfied I was getting my own share of bites/strikes and fish. I'll tell you some of the things I learned in another chapter. I will say it was worth listening to Shorty. He may not have made a contribution to the war effort. I don't know. But he did add to my happy memories.

I can visualize him today, standing on the lakefront near Gramps' shack, looking out across the lake and watching the fish rise. He wore a beat-up fedora with an old jacket and nondescript pants. I imagine him with a not-quite-vacant look on his ordinary face – not smiling, not frowning, but with just a hint of an expression that may have said he was looking for someone to listen to something he had to tell.

— The Old Gray Building —

When I first went to work for Gramps at the boathouse, the entire shoreline of American Lake was a wonderful mystery to me. I recall my excitement when I thought about the job, before I'd ever glimpsed the lake itself.

For some reason I thought of Lake Washington when the name of American Lake first came up. This is probably not too startling a mistake from a young boy who had seldom been away from home overnight up to that time. I erroneously imagined the lake where I would be working as located on saltwater or, miraculously, on both salt and fresh water. This allowed me to imagine my semi-heroic figure on a large dock doing something in relation to fish with the brand new large knife we boys had each received at Christmas from our uncles, along with rudimentary fishing outfits. I imagined doing necessary chores for fishermen with that marvelous knife, perhaps using the serrated second blade to scale someone's catch.

I did not know that Lake Washington was in the other direction, up by Seattle, and that it, too, was freshwater, although connected to Puget Sound via locks. It was also much larger than American Lake – a matter of 19 miles long versus three and a half.

But I was far from disappointed when I first saw the lake that was to be my happy homesite for many days. There was so much to take in that I could not absorb it all at once.

After I had learned the path down the hill, past the privy on the left and between the two Gawley-owned houses, to the bottom where Grandpa's shack and the docks were located, I gradually started to understand where things were.

Looking both to the left or south and to the right or north, one could see beachfront homes one next to another with hardly a break. These structures stood between two points of land that jutted out into the lake a short distance between a gently sloping shoreline. Most of the homes seemed to have docks or boathouses and several had extensive beautiful green lawns running up to houses set back from the lake itself.

Tall evergreen trees dominated the skyline and were interspersed with a variety of deciduous trees, maples and others. Even with the keen eyes of youth, I could not make out from our dock the sign on the point to the south that warned, "Boats beyond this point subject to military control."

Because of the war, people were jumpy, and stories of saboteurs and spies being landed on the nation's coasts were not rare. The land south of the point was, indeed, under military control as part of Fort Lewis. As I learned later, soldiers in Jeeps patrolled the road that hugged the shore of the area we came to call The Soldiers' Beach.

Further to the south and beyond my sight and imagination at the time was Little American Lake, the smaller body of water that was connected to the lake proper by a shallow and narrow channel. At that time, a bridge built of unpainted logs and timbers by the soldiers of the Engineer Training Center at the fort spanned this channel. On weekends, soldiers killing time relaxed by walking over the bridge to the buildings, tennis court, swimming and other facilities the Army had built on a short peninsula creeping from the west between the two bodies of water.

Medical Care for Vets

If I looked due west from Don's boathouse across the lake, Silcox Island dominated the picture. We will get back to describing this colorful wooded piece of land rising from the lake. Beyond the island my attention was caught right away by yellow buildings set back a short distance from the lake's west side. These were part of a large and sprawling government veterans' hospital.

A bit north of the hospital grounds I could make out a large gray structure. It was too far away to see in detail, but it piqued my interest because it was unusual. The buildings of the hospital were interesting enough, but I rapidly fit them into a place in my mind. Besides, they looked almost identical to one another at a distance. But the great gray building was one of a kind.

It was a while before I grew at ease rowing the boats from Don's. I had never rowed anything before. But I rapidly learned and got a lot of practice. In fact, it was not long before I ventured to row across the big lake right up to the gray building.

My chance came one day after a fairly severe windstorm that made the waves slop rhythmically up against the dock where my sleeping room was located. It was just another restful night's sleep to me, but when I got up in the morning and had wolfed down a breakfast of pancakes, fried eggs, and bacon with Grandpa, he gave me a special job to do.

"The wind took away one of our boats last night," he said. "I want you to take one of the boats and see if you can row around the lake and find it."

That suited me fine. I liked to row, and I would have another chance to explore the fascinating shoreline. The prevailing wind was from the south, so it made sense to start to the north. This meant crossing the lake just to my right of the island as I faced it from the boathouse.

So I took a boat, probably number 16 or 17 and surely not one of the plywood boats stacked diagonally on the smaller dock. Then I removed the two cement anchors and anchor ropes from the boat and left them on the shore by Gramps' shack. No need to carry more weight than I had to. But I also took a length of rope with me to secure the lost boat when and if I found it.

Our Fishing Flotilla

I mentioned taking either number 16 or 17 as my choice. It would have been better, perhaps, to take No. 3 or one of the other two round-bottomed boats tied to the smaller dock. They cut the water better than the other boats. I always thought one of our regular customers, a Mr. Frank Lee, was not too sharp because he always rented No. 3. But he was a troller, contrary to the practices of just about everyone else at the time. So he opted for a boat that was easier to row.

Years later, I learned that trolling for the trout and kokanee in the lake was productive and had other advantages over stillfishing as we practiced it.

But why No. 16 or 17? Silly reasons, I am sure. Ever since I was a toddler, the number 6 was my favorite and blue was my favorite color. I also liked the numbers 2 and 9. The reason I opted for six was that cowboys had six-shooters. Makes sense, huh? But why 16? I suppose because it had a six in it. At the time, I could not have known that I would be wearing No. 16 on my uniform as I played on our high school baseball team.

Why people prefer one number or color to others is a mystery to me. So it came down to either No. 16 or 17. The boats had some individuality even though they were similar. I liked 16 for whatever reasons and I liked 17 because it was nearly identical.

But there was one difference between 16 and 17. Someone had carved the word FART on the back seat of No. 17. Each winter Gramps painted most or all of the boats green. Numbers were stenciled on the bows and repairs were made as needed. Gramps also inspected and replaced worn anchor lines and made new anchors from cement in old coffee cans. And when he painted the boats, he painted over the sizeable inscription on No. 17, but he did not fill it.

Once a man came in to rent a boat on a day when I had charge of the operation. He paid his fee and requested "that boat with FART on the seat."

As I rowed across the lake, I kept to the north side of the island where there were several small homes in the woods with docks on their waterfronts. I saw to the left more of the buildings of the hospital, hinting at its giant size.

As I approached a point of land poking out into the lake, I was able to discern the gray building in some detail. Its color was the result of its wood structure bleaching in the sun for many years. And as I stroked closer I could see that it had no roof and that some boards were hanging down from rafters and swinging in the breeze.

Now, I have never been over-inquisitive when it comes to anything requiring exploratory courage. It is my nature to be content with knowing part of a mystery's solution and to wait for a possible windfall of more information at a later date. So I did not even consider going ashore and exploring the building. The floor could have proved treacherous or some of that great gray thing could have come tumbling down on me. In other words, I was chicken.

Had I known what I learned much later, I could have listened for the echoes of men and women relaxing and celebrating in what seemed to be a very old version of a roadhouse. I learned that the old street car's rails used to run out to the building on North American Lake to transport Tacomans bent on entertainment.

Again, I was not inclined to play historian. Even today, that old building seems like a phantom of a bygone day that is still shrouded in mystery. Who was the owner? What kind of food and drink were served? Did earlier residents take their horses and buggies out to the lovely wooded lake, and did they stay overnight or just spend a few pleasant hours? I don't know.

I found the boat and tied a rope to it to pull it behind No. 16 back to the boathouse. Gramps would be pleased. And I had learned some geography and glimpsed a bit of history. Also, just to the south of the old building, I noticed a narrow and shallow inlet that looked intriguing but would have to wait for another day for exploration because I had a long row back.

— Chubby and Butch —

If living at American Lake, helping Grandpa and getting to go fishing every day was near enough to Heaven for me, it was more so because of Chubby and Butch.

I have always taken a dim view of a vision of Heaven without lots of dogs and cats and other creatures as well. But my love of dogs certainly got a boost because the two canines owned by the Gawleys shared just about every day with Grandpa and me.

Actually I can't give Butch much credit for attendance. He was around the premises but he kept to himself a lot. In those days people let their dogs roam, but I don't think he had a wanderlust. Like me, he probably had everything he desired on the boathouse property, so he must have spent a lot of time napping in the shadows of the two houses up the hill.

As for Chubby, she was just a bundle of love. As soon as she and Butch were let out in the morning, she bolted down the hill to see what Gramps and I were up to. She nosed around the plywood shack and counted the customers for us. When we ate breakfast, she sometimes came in to have a few bites with us.

Sweets for the Sweet One

One morning while I was eating breakfast of bacon and pancakes, Chubby sat near my chair with her tongue hanging out. I, of course, responded with a bite or two of pancake, but she didn't seem overwhelmed by the handout. "Put a little honey on it," Grandfather said, and I did.

Since I was up before daylight and usually out on the lake fishing first thing, there were many mornings when Chubby must have wondered where I was. It is a good thing she didn't spot me out in a boat anchored maybe fifty yards out where the springs were. Because if she had, I would have had to pull her up into the boat after she swam out to join me.

The reason I know that would have happened was based on my observation of Chubby's habits.

She was a typical cocker spaniel, a little bit overweight as her name indicated. She was a beautiful reddish color, not identical to but not far from the color often seen on Irish setters.

I did not know her age, but she had to be a young dog because of all her exuberance.

One mid-morning I decided to head south up the lake in pursuit of some fisherman's idea. It was only when I had gone perhaps seventy-five yards toward the military sign that I realized I was being followed. There was Chubby, somewhat astern and paddling in dead earnest as her long ears drooped along beside like demoted outriggers.

I put on the brakes and hauled a heavily soaked little dog up into the boat. She had impressed me with her speed and strength as a swimmer, and I was flattered that she wanted to be with me.

Perils of Butch

In the meantime, Butch was doing his own thing. He was on a pinnacle of joy when he could get out on the smaller dock and try to catch the half-tame mallards that swam regally in the channel between the two docks.

He would bark and edge right up to the water, then pull back a few steps and plunge forward again to repeat his charge. One could imagine a spring recoiling before one more run to the brink. Then, suddenly, his tactics got out of hand or paw and he would leap out into the channel and come up sputtering. Pit bulls, which is what Butch was, were not bred for swimming. He must have inhaled lots of water, judging by all the noise and spray.

On shore without a duck or even a duck feather, Butch seemed non-repentant. He was doomed like Sisyphus to roll his rock up the hill without reward. Only his hill was mallard ducks.

Here I would like to comment that Butch seemed to be far from the vicious pit bulls we read about in the papers today. He was like the dog Pete that Spanky McFarlane and his gang had in their movies. From this I reinforce my belief that there are few if any bad dogs but a lot of bad owners. The Gawleys were good owners, so I am sure Butch got a lot of love and care.

His morals were apparently not high. I base this observation on a remark Larry Feir made to me the day after I returned to the lake from my day off in town. "Did you see old Butch in action?" Larry asked. Apparently a female dog or two had wandered by the boathouse in an amorous mood. Butch was said to have acted like the typical Hollywood actor or TV evangelist. Naughty boy!

Another time, Larry or someone else told me that Butch was down by the shore while someone was casting a big bass plug from the small dock. The story went that Butch got hooked in the side but had sense enough to let the offending humans unhook him. I was glad I missed that event.

Chubby spent some time with us on the big dock as we caught our share of the perch attempting to spawn that spring. We had to watch our hooks so as to avoid the inquisitive dog. She must have thought we were crazy to let those fish flop around on the dock instead of leaving them where they belonged down below the planks.

Eggs and Quackers

We were doubly careful after an incident with an overfriendly mallard drake.

The mallards were at least half tame because people fed them sandwich crumbs and other tidbits and few people if any would stoop to molest them. They were a joy to watch as they led their ducky lives, and we pretty much ignored them except when

Mama Duck proudly led her small fleet of ducklings nearby as they learned how to swim and eat and behave like ducks.

But this one time, we had left our bamboo poles leaning against the roof overhang of the little dock building, and we had neglected to strip off the salmon eggs we used for bait.

First thing we knew, there was a big strong duck flying in circles overhead with a hook and salmon eggs in its beak. Jim let the bird fly a few laps and then as gently as possible worked his line in. We cut the leader near the protesting mallard and it plowed away from us indignantly. We hoped and trusted the duck was not hurt, but as I mentioned, it made us more cautious after that.

There is not a lot more to say here about Chubby and Butch. I lost track of them as time went on and the Gawleys sold out and moved. But as long as they were there, they added to my enjoyment of the American Lake years, and I am sure Jim would second that.

Brother Paul who succeeded me for a couple of years as boathouse boy enjoyed Chubby as well. Anyone would love a pretty little pleasingly plump cocker like Chubby.

Louis and brother Billy Paul in front of the house with a catch of "silvers" from American Lake.

— How We Got to Heaven —

It was our great good fortune that Grandpa Seidelman found employment with the Gawleys at American Lake. He must have been close to 65 years old at the time and most Americans then aspired to retire at that age. The Gawleys could not hope to hire someone in his 30s or 40s, so they settled on the old man. He was remarkable as a physical specimen at his age and was perfectly capable of doing all he was required to do in running the boathouse.

Had it not been for Grandpa's employment, our lives would have been quite different. There were few paying jobs for boys under the age of 16, so I would have probably continued playing ball every day of the summer and picking up a little change by mowing lawns or other rare odd jobs.

Tickets, Please

Gas was a scarce item during the war years. Many families had yet to emerge from a Depression time when many did not have a family car. So we rode buses or pedaled bicycles or walked to wherever we needed to go.

American Lake seemed to be a long way from home, although the boathouse was only about 12 miles from my cozy room overlooking the cherry tree. So there had to be a way to get from there to here and vice versa. Fortunately, there was.

We lived right on M Street, an important arterial in our neck of the woods. The bus stopped on the corner of 41st and M, a corner that fronted the only undeveloped lot on our block. Our place was right next to the corner, so I was able to swoop down the front concrete steps in front of Grandma's and catch the South Tacoma bus on its way downtown. Or, conversely, we could cross M Street and stand on the corner in front of the

Liberty Lumber Yard to head to South Tacoma. Either way, we could make a connection to a bus that would take us to American Lake.

Going downtown, one got a transfer so as to continue riding after a switch to one of the many other city bus routes. If one were headed to American Lake, a ride all the way to the end of the South Tacoma line at Fawcett Park – the one graced with a drinking fountain and the old Indian totem pole – took the rider to within a scant block of the Interurban Station at 8th and A Streets. This building served Greyhound and the Lake Shore Stage Line, both of which were separate from the city buses and required separate fares. Army buses to and from Fort Lewis also used the same terminal building.

The buses that took us to the lake were usually crowded with riders, most of them people going to and from employment. So it was wise to catch the bus at the terminal to make it likely one would get a seat for the long ride. Jim and I expected to stand, but we liked to get on early anyway because we were afraid there might not be space for us at all.

Sometimes I crossed M Street and took the bus that terminated at South Tacoma Way and South 52nd St., where one could stand under the canopy of Ludwig's Drugstore. Then it was a matter of crossing South Tacoma Way and walking a block to South 54th. There Jim and I stood outside the North Pacific Bank's brick facade and waited for the Lake Shore Stage bus to appear from the north on its way from downtown.

Jim lived near South 56th and I Streets, so he could walk a few blocks from home and get on the South Tacoma bus at 56th and M. Like as not, I would be on the same bus that I had caught from in front of Liberty Lumber a few minutes before.

Pardon Me, Madam

This all may sound easy, but there was a complicating factor. We had to take our fishing tackle and sometimes items such as sleeping bags and food along with us. We were no day tourists, but rather a couple of explorers bent on staying for at least one night in pursuit of trout and spiny ray fishes.

The buses were packed to capacity, but despite our fears, we were never turned away by the understanding drivers. The people who had been at work for a day had to put up with two teenagers sometimes wrestling big sleeping bags and usually carrying wicker creels and fishing poles. My creel was old and it smelled of old fish, but I never recall anyone objecting to our crowding in with the rest of the folks. When we caught the bus in South Tacoma, we stood all the way to the lake except in rare cases.

As long as we had access to the room on the dock, we had the best of situations. We could leave our sleeping bags in the room and not have to wrestle them through crowds of adults on the bus. Just take them out to the lake once and home once more at the end of fishing season.

The Lake Shore Line bus continued southward through South Tacoma along South Tacoma Way, which was the main highway at that time. We looked for landmarks such as the place near Clover Creek where a main road crossed the highway on an overpass. Then Clover Creek itself fanned our imaginations – could we someday slosh up that weedy and overgrown streambank to see if there were any lovely speckled fish hiding in the shadows and waiting for our angle worms?

A little further and we were at Ponders' Corner, a small historic accumulation of businesses including the Aba Daba Cafe. On the way home from the lake one could hardly miss the huge neon sign near the cafe that promoted Olympia beer. A few years later when I was a GI at Fort Lewis starting a weekend pass, I knew my home was getting closer when I saw the comforting Oly sign through the bus window.

The bus to the lake left the highway at Thorne Lane and swept along the flank of the lake past Firch's Boathouse and, on the left, a kind of country store/trading post place. I never went in there because I had no money to spend. I recall we got off the bus at this store and hoofed it the rest of the short way to the boathouse.

Near that building there were logs fashioned in such a manner that one could sit upon them while waiting for the bus without getting slivers from their use-polished surface. Unless it were raining, this was a comfortable place to wait for the bus going either way.

After the bus dumped us, it turned to the left and headed east to the highway again. On the other side of the highway there was a housing project, either for GIs or defense workers or both. This place was called American Lake Gardens. Once I heard an adult say to someone else, "Huh, American Lake Gardens. There isn't a tree in the whole place."

Between Two Homes

As the summer progressed, I began to realize that I was fortunate to have two great places to stay: on the one hand, in Tacoma, my beautiful room with a view, mother in the kitchen cooking up a panoply of delicious food, our pet dog Tiny, the nearby ballfield; and on the other hand, my waterborne room on the dock with fish under and all around, the colorful Coke sign, and a cot with sleeping bag on it.

I was truly fortunate, and the best thing was that I knew how blessed I was from the get-go.

As Jim and I traveled back and forth to the lake, even our waiting hours were not boring. We always had a lot to talk about. School: Jim took chemistry before I did and he explained it as well as he could to me. He had a theory that he could see life in terms of salts and bases and acids. I struggled to understand but did not catch up until I took chemistry in my junior year at Lincoln. Even then, his theory baffled me.

We talked of sports and girls, male friends, and which teachers we liked and did not like and why. Mostly, we talked fishing. The time flew.

I recall waiting in front of the North Pacific Bank with Jim early one morning. We were primed to fish as soon as possible, since we knew early morning was the best time. Jim eyed a tank of tropical fish in the bank window.

"Boy, look at how active those fish are," Jim exclaimed. "I bet they'll be biting like crazy." We could hardly stand the suspense.

If there had been a bus at 3 a.m., we would have been on it.

Some years later, we slept one night on the dock outside the locked room. I do not recall why we were out rather than in, but there had to be a reason. No matter. In order to get an early jump on fishing, we gladly tried to sleep on the hard planks. It was not easy for two keyed-up fishermen.

"I Know a Guy"

There were other ways to get to the lake for early morning fishing though these were only occasional chances. We grasped them all with eagerness.

Frankie K. was as crazy about fishing as we were. We swapped tales with him when we saw him. One day he told us he knew a guy who would give two or three of us a lift to the lake early. This could benefit all of us. Gramps would let us use a boat without charge, and we could get a free early ride to the lake.

It seems Frankie knew a truck driver who delivered pies and other pastries early to the Olympia area, south of Tacoma. The truck driver happened to be named Frank, too. Turns out he was a fellow teamster and friend of our Uncle Oscar, Mother's older brother, who introduced brother Billy Paul and me to fishing.

We caught a ride with Frank a few times, but he stopped for his breakfast along the way, which made us antsy. But we did not push our needs with him. We had some change for a cup of coffee, since we saved bus fare riding with Frank, so we could go into a restaurant with him and he did not dawdle over his meal. After all, he had a schedule to make.

A New Denomination

There was one time when we rode with Frank that we had a real adventure. My brother Paul and I still talked of it after more than 70 years. Sherlock Holmes would have called it The Case of the Lincoln-Head Dollars.

We could hear the sirens in the distance. The cops are closing in on somebody, we thought as we sipped our coffee and Frank ate some breakfast. There was a chuckle and we became aware for the first time of someone sitting on one of the counter stools.

"They're probably looking for me," a scrawny young fellow in an Army uniform said. He had scratches and dried blood on his forehead and ears, and his GI tie was loosely draped around a shirt opened a button or two at the top. He was definitely out of uniform. Any MP would have picked him up for that alone, but there were more serious charges pending.

It seemed the young private had spent virtually all of his weekend pass time and most of his money playing poker in a South Tacoma residence.

He warmed his hand on the coffee mug and proceeded to tell us about the ebb and flow of a game without end. It was then that I noticed for the first time that his left arm hung limply at his side, but he seemed able to pump enough heat through the good hand to warm his whole body.

"These other fellows were Filipinos," he said. Then he noticed us looking at his arm. "I think it's broken," he said. But this did not seem to temper his upbeat attitude. "There was one hell of a fight after that big sergeant accused that little Filipino dealer of cheating.

"Someone upset the table and there was chips and money and glasses flying all over the place. Those little Filipinos were fast and tough as nails. I got knocked down right away and under the table. Someone kicked me right in the ribs. But I just picked up another Lincoln-head dollar and stuffed it in my shirt.

"Right away I could see that was the thing to do. Every time anyone hit or kicked me, I just picked up another Lincoln-head dollar and put it in my shirt."

After some broken furniture and some bones, too, he bounced down a flight of stairs near the front door. He didn't remember landing a single punch in the fracas, but he did take quite a beating. The term stuffed shirt took on a whole new meaning as he kept smiling through his pain.

We boys sipped our coffee while Frank finished off his breakfast. The soldier resumed his tale. He said sirens were beginning to wail in the distance, so our man – he had become our man as he cheerfully spun out his tale – grabbed his Army cap and limped away up the street. About then another early exiter from the poker game swung by in an old Ford and opened the car door without much of a perceptible stop. "Get in and we'll get the hell out of here."

Our man was dumped at a bus stop, which happened to be near the cafe where Frank had stopped for his breakfast. So he looked at the neon sign atop the little place and thought it looked friendly. It was only then that he realized something was not right with his left arm. He chuckled to himself, took a wad of bills from his shirt, stuffed them into his pants pocket, and decided to get some breakfast. "Those little guys were sure fast," he said.

Early to Bed, Etc.

On one of our trips with Frank the bakery driver, we had an epiphany of sorts. The time was near 4 a.m. and we boys were not about to miss our rendezvous with Frank, so we got up early enough for breakfast and bathroom trips. We didn't think much about it. That is what you did if you were a fisherman: Get up early and get your bait in the water before the other guys.

We were to meet Frank at South 48th and M, so three or four of us trudged along the sidewalk moving south on the east side of M. But as we passed a house near the corner of 45th and M, we were startled to hear and see several adults coming out a front door. The lights of the interior burst out into the dark street and the air tinkled with the laugh of some lady who had a drink or two.

The adults were as startled as we. "What are you guys doing up at this hour?" someone asked. We explained and they laughed when we expressed amazement that they were apparently just going to bed as we were starting out on our fishing trip.

It made us think a little. Were there really people who lived like that? Seemed there were. And nice folks, too. They came across friendly as they laughed at our explanations.

They must have thought we were strange kids. Who would get up at such an ungodly time to try to catch some slimy fish? Guess who.

So that was pretty much it. Catch a city bus, then a Lakeshore Stage Lines bus and hoof it a short distance to the lake. Or get a ride from a friendly truck driver who had not forgotten how it felt to be a kid.

American Lake with all those fish seemed to be the end of the rainbow or paradise to me. There was gainful employment, adventure, and fish to take home to Mom once a week. Would any Rockefeller care to trade places with me?

— A Commando Operation —

It was cool in the morning when I slid out of bed well before sunrise and pulled on my cords and T shirt. The temperature did not bother me. My room at home would not have been much warmer, but such details were easily shrugged off. Too, getting up so early was no problem to a boy who loved to fish and who believed that the best time to catch fish was early in the morning.

In fact, we – my friend Jim and I – were neurotic about fishing early. When we started to get our first baits down to the silvers, it was often not easy to discern the tip of the rod because it was still the dark of night. By 8 a.m., the fishing day was over as far as we were concerned.

Grandpa would still be sleeping in his little green shack on the shore as I walked across the gangway. He worked long hours and was physically active for a man of his years, so he cherished the hours and minutes he spent beneath the blankets before waking to reach under his bed for the ever-present bottle of schnapps. Following his eye-opener, he started a fire in the wood stove and pulled on his outer clothes over the longjohns he slept in. Then he made a trip up the hill to the privy that was dug into the earth near the base of the big Douglas fir we used as a landmark to line up our fishing efforts.

But it would be a while before the old man would have to roll out today. Unless an ambitious fisherman came down the hill and knocked on the shack door to rent a boat, John could sleep in as late as 5 a.m., perhaps. Then it would be time enough to face the world once more.

Up the Creek Silently

Putting on my Keds and slipping into my letterman's jacket with the leather sleeves, I slung my wicker creel over my shoulder and hit the trail up the hill, pausing briefly at the privy to do the usual and to look out over the darkness of the mirror-like lake.

Then it was up to the road at the top and full steam ahead toward the highway to the east. I carried my flyrod assembled and ready for fishing. A number nine egg hook was embedded in the cork handle of the rod. The four-pound leader had two or three split shot sinkers pinched onto it. A jar of salmon eggs and a plastic container with angle worms in it rested in the creel. My fishing knife in my back pants pocket made me feel a little like a commando ready to step onto a French beach in the dark of night.

I did not know if there were cause to hide from view as much as possible, but my mission was a secret one, and there was no sense in taking unnecessary chances. So I moved along swiftly and silently toward the objective past the Barbecue Inn on the left and through the few houses of the little village of Tillicum that clung to the higher ground above the lake.

Soon I was at the highway. I turned to my right toward the south, keeping to the grass and brush. Then I looked both ways along the two-lane highway and when I saw no cars, I quickly cut across the hard surface of the pavement.

But before I could get across to the other side, a car came from the Tacoma direction and the driver honked several times at me. After all, what the hell was a young kid doing in the middle of the highway at such an early hour?

I hoped no one else would see me as I moved along a short distance to the south along another grassy and brushy strip beside the roadway. Now there was need for stealth. Murray Creek ran under the highway, coming from Fort Lewis to the east. Somewhere I had learned that the creek, which I knew emptied into American Lake, had to be very near to my highway-crossing point.

A Small Invasion

Suddenly I saw it through the morning mist. Right away, I could see that my objective was protected. A small guard station illuminated by a single light bulb stood near the highway and right next to the creek. Years later when I was in the Army at Fort Lewis and was pulling guard duty, I was able to appreciate more than likely what was going on. A lonely young GI, or perhaps two guys, were keeping as warm as they could in the little structure. They were probably looking at magazines or talking about their high school days. If you told them a teenage kid with a lethal-looking spear or fishing pole was lurking nearby in the brush, you would have made them laugh.

But I did not know all this. I just knew that I wanted to see if I could catch a trout from the creek. So I sneaked along the bank of the little stream and dropped a juicy worm on my hook into a likely looking spot or two. No takers. The creek was quite anemic at this time of year – hardly enough water to hold trout worthy of the trouble.

My expedition was coming to an end. It was getting lighter and the traffic on the highway was increasing. So I sneaked back the way I had come and trotted homeward, the Barbecue Inn on my right this time. I felt no sense of accomplishment from my raid on the perimeter of Fort Lewis, but I had satisfied my curiosity about the possibility of worthy fish in the creek.

Back at the lake, I quickly passed over the gangplank to my home dock. Smoke was coming out of the tin stovepipe in Gramps' shack. He would be cooking up something good for breakfast. And he would not have noticed that I was gone. On many mornings I slipped into one of our boats and rowed out to fish over the springs. After awhile, Gramps would come out on the dock and yell at me that breakfast was ready.

If the fishing was good, it was hard to hear him. But this morning after my hike, I was ready for pancakes or fried potatoes. Life was good partly because of breakfast.

I opened the padlock to my room and put my creel inside. The pole I propped up against the wall of the building. No need to put it away: No one would take it and I would be using it again in a few minutes or an hour or two at the most.

Jim would be coming out on the bus and there were perch and rock bass to catch through the hole in the dock. But I sure would have liked to tell him about the several nice trout I caught up in Murray Creek under the noses of the guards.

They were really beauties.

Louis taking a break from building an escort carrier.

— Castle with a Wide Moat —

We are brought up on stories and history studded with romantic islands. American Lake certainly owes a good deal of its charm to Silcox Island. There are four smaller islets. Two of them figure into my memories, but the other two are so swallowed up by the National Guard facility at Camp Murray that they might as well not be there.

How about those Dorothy Lamour movies and Treasure Island, Mutiny on the Bounty, and many other island movies?

Islands sparkle in those tales like rare jewels in their watery setting. Before reaching Tahiti or Pitcairn, a perilous journey over the deep is required. And once there, exotic pleasures are to be expected.

Although I have never set foot on Silcox Island, I did get an invitation at least once. Jim and I memorized the shoreline of the 13-acre beauty, but we never seriously thought of landing there for any purpose. The island grew in my imagination into a sort of inviolable castle. Who lived there and what was it like to peer through the trees and other foliage from a high point on the island to glimpse the fishing boats and scullers and seagulls and ducks on the clear surface? We never found out because we were brought up under rules that discouraged trespass. Besides, one could hear dogs barking from time to time as we made our way around the shoreline.

A World Apart

What lay hidden behind the thick forest on the island was a mystery to me until a writer named Bart Ripp did some research and came up with a number of facts, for which I am grateful. By and large the information in the March 28, 1997, issue of the Tacoma News Tribune appears to be accurate, although Ripp gives two separate figures for the purchase price of the island: $305 and $350. Mr. A.A. Silcox ponied up one of those figures in 1905 and promptly named the forested beauty for himself. I do recall that someone within my hearing said the entire island was for sale during the war years for $100,000. This seems reasonable in view of other land values at the time, but it cannot be verified.

It appears there are about 25 homes on the island. These line the entire shoreline, and almost all include docks for the mooring of speedboats, sailboats, canoes, exotic craft including amphibious Amphicars, and some floatables looking more like docks with outboard motors attached than boats.

A historical description of one residence on the island included: a gabled roof, a turret with seven windows, a gazebo, goldfish ponds, and wild transplanted rhododendrons from the Olympic Peninsula. Jim and I never felt we saw anything that luxurious from our rowboat, but there is one place on the northern shore that has a castle-like turret.

Meeting a Ghostly Forest

There is nothing like fog to shroud the prosaic in mystery. When Jim and I first looked west across the lake, we could not help but see the large forested island that we knew stood between us and the Veterans' Hospital on the far shore of the lake.

There was a treat in store for us on a foggy June morning when we took one of the Gawley boats on an early fishing outing that turned out to be a voyage of discovery.

It took only a few minutes to get lost in the fog. First, the docks of the boathouse melted into grayness. The big trees further up the hill were already hiding in blankets of mist.

It is easy to get turned around in the fog on a lake as large as American. A few times I have started out from a launching area and was startled to find myself back at the launch in just a few minutes. The intent had been to be somewhere else across the lake. But that day we were close enough to the island so that we did not miss its fringe completely. Once in sight of shore – sort of – we kept close enough to land so that we could proceed around the island, meanwhile making clumsy efforts to fish.

Rube Goldberg, Angler

I allude to the fishing here because it illustrates something about fishing in general that I believe is true: Don't get caught up in making things more complicated than they are.

I had whittled a little plug, or what I felt a plug should be, out of a piece of scrap wood. Painted yellow with red spots, it was ugly enough to catch a fish, had it been rigged up to negotiate water in any semblance of a piece of fishing tackle. But that was not good enough for Jim and me – I drag Jim in on this to share our mutual shame at the idiocy of it all – we had to complicate things by rigging up lines and leaders so that the little ugly plug appeared to be chasing two larger hooks that were loaded with three or four juicy salmon eggs each.

I am sure the first trout that saw our setup quickly dived to the bottom of the lake where it squatted on a bar stool and tried to forget the whole thing. I have seen fish caught in some strange manners, but not that strange.

Nonetheless, we trailed our monstrosity around the island behind us. I do not recall what Jim had on his hook. Probably a worm or part of a worm or a suitable covering of salmon eggs. At any rate, he had a hell of a lot better chance of catching a trout than I.

So we followed the shoreline all the way around the island and we agreed that it was a pretty thing. Also, we marveled at the spooky feeling we got when we strayed a little far from the island shore and got lost for a minute or two. A Loch Ness monster could have been about to rise to the surface. But at last the sun rose higher and the mist dissipated. We could see the boathouse and the eastern lake shore where Grandfather was cooking up something for breakfast and Chubby and Butch were about to charge down the hill.

Lady of the Lake

Perhaps you recall the fanciful story about King Arthur and the Lady of the Lake. She was supposed to have thrust an immaculately groomed arm – the left one, I believe – up through the surface of a lake in order to present young Arthur with his marvelous sword. A good tale, perhaps to be improved only by the voluptuous arm offering not a sword but a perfectly balanced flyrod attached to a decent single-action reel with a good-quality flyline included in the gift.

There was no submerged maiden arising from American Lake, and there was no gift, either sword or flyrod. However, we had something better: someone lovely and half mysterious.

Perhaps there was nothing much mysterious about Dorothy Johnson. Any mystery was probably just the bashful observations of a 14-year-old boy. I am sure Jim, too, was equally overwhelmed by the sight of Dorothy as she steered her red canoe up to our beach, where she landed after her trip to the mainland from her home on the island.

Dorothy was beautiful. She was a young blonde, perhaps 19 or 20 years old, with a perfect full figure. She paddled her canoe in an expert manner, back and forth almost every day and sometimes more than once a day.

I recall one time when she made at least two trips in one day. To her credit, I never heard her swear. In that ancient time, ladies were not often provoked to swear.

It was after our suppertime. We ate early, probably about 5 p.m. This was a habit developed from being a teenage boy who burned up many calories a day, often in athletic endeavors and from constant and vigorous walking and running. Many times I had to ask my mother whether we had eaten yet, sometimes not long after a meal. Typically I would be at death's door from starving about 5:02 and Mom would assure me the meal would be forthcoming "as soon as the potatoes get through boiling." Grandfather was apparently like-minded, so we ate early.

It was after suppertime, probably on a Friday or Saturday. I say this because Dorothy was dressed to the nines when she ran her canoe a few inches up our partly sandy beach. She stepped out of her chariot, a goddess, a real Heaven-sent angel that lived on a misty island, when . . .

The Cruelty of Fate

My God, Dorothy had a run in her stocking! This was no trivial matter. To magnify the seriousness, silk stockings were not easy to get or replace in this war year.

Nothing to do but climb back in the canoe and paddle swiftly back to her home on the island. She did what she had to and repaired the cruel happening while probably setting an untimed Olympics best paddling record from the boathouse to the island and back.

Either my grandfather or I were on hand to grab the canoe prow and pull it up on the sand. On other occasions, Grandfather had joked with Dorothy. "If I was twenty years younger I would ask you out myself," the old man said. "And if you were twenty years younger I would probably say yes," the good-natured girl said.

But after the run in the stocking, time did not allow for badinage. Dorothy was out of the canoe a second time and up the hill. I never knew, but there must have been a Johnson car parked at the top. Either that or Dorothy sprouted a pair of wings and flew off, like the angel she was, toward town.

It was many years after that I found out Dorothy was the granddaughter of A. A. Silcox and that she had lived all her life up to that point on the island. She married Clary Holm, a friend of my older brother Jack, and the Holms continued to live on the island. In a telephone conversation with Clary some years ago before his death, he invited me to come out to see him at the island. I wish I had, but to this date have never set foot on the island. It seems Clary was working on a history of Silcox Island,

and he was interested in my experience as Grandfather's boatboy.

A few more facts about Silcox Island with thanks to Mr. Ripp, who did restaurant reviews and some other writing for the Tacoma paper. I never met him, even though I also did reviews and other editorial tasks for years for the same newspaper.

Facts in Passing

Albert Abner Silcox, Dorothy's grandfather, was reputedly an intimidating figure. He stood six feet two, and was known as a rough-talking customer. He built a family residence and other buildings on the island and rented some places to vacationers. A newspaper ad in 1911 said: "Ask for A. A. Silcox at the old house where the flag is flying."

Silcox, an Ontario native of English heritage, purchased the island from Tacoma Land Co. Before settling on the island, he had cleared land and had run a small furniture store in Tacoma, in addition to doing odd jobs.

Five of the approximately 25 residences on the island are occupied year round. One place on the northwest shore became a home to the Totem Ski Club. Most of the places sit quietly and await the family picnics, barbecues, and vacation outings of summer.

The expanse of lake to the western shore from the island is at least twice as far as from the boathouse side. The island's north side often becomes the lee side as prevailing winds come in from the south. On the north side there is an underwater shelf extending for some distance where the water depth is about 40 feet and level. Further to the north and to the west, the depths reach more than 90 feet in places.

The water around the island drops off rather abruptly. Rowing around the island near the shoreline, one finds himself looking up at the large firs and madronas, rather than eyeing them more or less on the level. It appears as if the island is more than a little like the top of a small mountain, another gift of the great sheet of ice that once covered the land here.

Four Dots on a Map

There are four other islands in American Lake and I have been near them often, but I don't know which name applies to which island and precisely where two of the four are located. The names of the islets are Beard, Barlow, Cors, and Short. The reason for all this uncertainty is that two of these islands are apparently tucked into the area just south of Murray Creek, which is controlled by the National Guard. Moored boats, small buildings and parked recreational vehicles make a hodge-podge that just seems like a mess as viewed from the lake. There is no reason to frequent this area. The surrounding water is too shallow and too busy to invite fishing.

The largest of the four islands is close to shore at the state boating access area. A second small island runs east and west and is located just south of the larger island. It has some small trees and shrubs on it, but is too small for any good use. A rocky bottom runs between these two islets, almost connecting them when the water is low. I have seen teenagers, boys and girls, picking their way through knee-deep water between the small islands during low water times. Usually, one can row a shallow draft boat such as a johnboat between the two islands, but this narrow passageway is not a good route with a motor.

An Overnight Frolic

The largest of the four islands is not large. I remember it as being maybe forty yards long at most – just a rusty estimate. But it eventually became the site of, I believe, two small summer homes.

Back in the, war years, there was no Game Department access near Murray Creek. The county road did not go down to the lake in those days. So anyone wanting to reach the four islands had to do so by boat. Four of us boys: Jim Hutson, Dick Tibbitts, Rich Hanson, and I, got our sleeping bags out to the boathouse, where we commandeered two of our favorite boats and rowed south past the military sign to the largest island.

Making camp was no complicated matter. We unrolled our sleeping bags on ground as level as we could find upon the eastern shore of the island. Then we collected enough dry wood to build a good fire on the rocky beach a few feet away. We had something to eat and talked a long time around the fire before making a night of it.

Dick Hanson had brought a jar of store-bought strawberry preserves which we all shared. There was a lot left over, and Dick tried to remedy that situation. So he ate too much of the sweet stuff and had the honor of being the first person to toss his cookies on our island retreat.

One of the good stillfishing spots in the lake where we caught any number of silvers and perch was halfway between the island and the point with the military sign. It is about 40 feet deep there and almost weed-free.

I don't recall the results of our fishing that day, but I know we had a good time. Often in those days we got skunked. Sometimes the fishing was poor. At other times we had not yet learned enough to figure out how best to go about our angling. At any rate, we were never surprised not to catch anything at all.

Years later, the State Game Department constructed the large public access with two cement ramps for fishermen. The road to the lake runs east and west alongside National Guard property. Before the terror attack of 9-11-01, the Guard permitted parking for trucks and boat trailers and other vehicles using the lake. This area of permission was quite large. Its loss greatly restricted parking for fishermen and others.

Shortly after 9-11, a tall wire fence was put up and access was cut off for civilian use of the area. Occasional patrols checked the perimeter from inside the fence. It appeared to me to be a typical over-reaction. I doubt many spies were lining up to attack Camp Murray.

But the ramps and part of the parking area remain. Kayakers and model airplane enthusiasts are among those joining shore anglers in using the lake. Annual fish plantings are made by the state using the ramps.

A few years ago as I was winding up a fishing trip with my boat on the ramp, I encountered a young man who was transporting sacks of cement and other building materials to the little island. I gave him a hand with some lifting and enjoyed talking with him. But, again, my lack of curiosity kept me from "picking his brains." Maybe he knew the name of his island, for example. I did not tell him how I had camped with my fishing buddies on his beach many years ago.

That this small island has a structure on it at all indicates how nature has been changed over the years. When Jim and I were doing our thing, this island and the nearby shore were brushy and forested. But in the intervening years, the nearby power company cottages have been replaced by condominiums or other structures. I know where they are but haven't the heart to go look at them. I'd rather remember them as they were when old Jock, the deaf care-taker, was there and when four high school-age boys could camp out on a rocky little island without thinking to ask permission.

— Wildlife Along the Shore —

My interest in fishing goes back much further than any interest in hunting. But, like most city kids, I have been fascinated by most animals that one finds in the wild. And it has been surprising how close to civilization many animals prosper.

So it was not a complete surprise to me when I saw a family of skunks on parade near the main buildings of the Soldiers' Beach one morning while fishing at the nearby logboom that provided shelter from wind and waves for the military boathouse operation.

Head up and marching with definite orders, mother skunk led three little black and white troopers along the shoreline. They worked their way to some brush, where they disappeared. I marveled at their confidence. No need for camouflage, just a reputation.

At the time I was not far from the place on the shore of the little lake where I had spotted a raccoon not long before. The only surprise here was that the little bandits are not seen more often. Back home in Tacoma it was not unheard of to see a raccoon or to become alarmed when hearing of someone's cat or dog being mauled by a fierce little robber in a residential neighborhood.

A Deer Here and There

It is a certainty that a lot more deer saw me than I saw them as I fished along the shoreline. But the silent approach in a rowboat or with an electric motor does give one an advantage over others who (1) make too much noise, (2) don't give a hoot about seeing animals, (3) don't know what to look for, and (4) don't know what they are looking at.

Much of the shoreline at the south end of the lake is still forested because it is part of the military holdings. The woods in places extend quite far from the lake and are teeming with deer, raccoons, porcupines, and assorted minklike creatures. There very likely are otters in American Lake but I have seen only muskrats. No beavers in my experience. Once Grandpa made reference to having seen a mink near our boats on the shore. That would have made sense. Little ducklings would please hungry minks.

I was delighted one summer's day to spy a large turtle sunning itself on a small float near the point with the military sign. I could not back off fast enough nor quietly enough, so I startled the creature and it slid into the depths. Never before nor since did I see a turtle in the lake.

It must have been someone's pet, because the cold lake would not be a hospitable place for native turtles. And its size – maybe roughly a foot in length – dwarfed any comparable creature I had even heard of, much less seen.

That turtle provided me a lot of food for thought over the years. I was alone when I saw it. There were no other witnesses. The turtle made no sound. Indeed, do turtles have even a tiny voice? I think not. The Biblical quote about the voice of the turtle being heard in the land obviously refers to the turtle dove.

Anyway, I thought about the old quote of a tree falling in the forest and no one hearing it. Was my mind – flexible or just plain weak – playing games with me? I wished for someone to share my experience with. Where was my friend Jim when I had something really different to show him?

Those two summers at the lake were largely spent with my own company. And I learned that I felt comfortable with myself as I thought over my experiences and options.

A Variety of Birds

Passing over the domestic animals, Chubby and Butch, one has to note the large number and variety of birds that enjoyed the summer days along with me. The mallard ducks patrolled the shoreline and seemed to always be close by, sometimes too close. They begged bites from anchored fishermen eating their lunches. Two or three drakes chased a younger male with much splashing as they sought the attention of a female duck.

The ducks nested along the shoreline of the south end of the lake. Each spring, proud mother ducks led their fuzzy little offspring along the shore and taught them how to eat bugs and to look cute.

The great blue herons also had nests here in the wilder expanses of shoreline, again to the south. A fisherman could almost always count on seeing a huge bird standing still on a snag near the shore. If the boat ventured too close, the big bird took off and spread its long wings, sometimes squawking loudly at the human intruder. In flight, the awkward bird was graceful as could be.

When I was working at the lake, no resident geese were obvious. But they moved in to nest and live in such numbers a few years ago that they became a nuisance. All over huge areas of Western Washington, people complained about large numbers of geese fouling docks and lawns with droppings.

The large Canada geese were impressive. A flight of them could contain 50 or more birds, and these huge numbers of birds invaded docks and yards. An early morning angler would see large numbers of geese sleeping with their heads tucked under their wings on the greenest lawns they could find.

Feathered Armada

One time a few years ago, I was headed toward the little lake on a fishing errand just as a group of geese came paddling its way north from the little lake. They were sailing through a narrow stretch between a log boom and the shore near where the two parts of the lake join. There were a half dozen or more proud parents and a large number of half-grown goslings.

I was concerned because some clowns in personal watercraft were not far away to the north. These, I thought, were perhaps the kind of people who run deer to death with snowmobiles. They might just enjoy disrupting the small armada. I held my breath and tried to position my own boat with my silent motor so that I might help to deter any such stupidity.

Fortunately, the geese made it to the larger expanse of lake, where the youngsters would have a better chance of making it into shallow water if they had to.

The state pretty much controlled the goose population. They used whatever methods they had. I believe they made most eggs in nests infertile as their best weapon. At any rate, there are not nearly so many geese today.

Mallard Hotel

The Army built two log booms near what used to be its recreational facility for enlisted men on a peninsula extending from the western shore toward the wooded shore to the east. These two bodies of land used to be linked with the old wooden bridge built by the soldiers at the Fort Lewis Engineer Training Center.

One of these log booms stretches the length of the small peninsula that used to contain a boathouse and Coke facility. Before these entities were closed up in favor of similar services on the other side of the peninsula – that is, in the little lake – this long boom provided protection from the weather for the boats and sailboats docked there. For a while there was a seaplane or two tethered nearby, but these were removed after someone (!) wrote a letter of protest to the local press.

The other log boom ran north and south at right angles to the first boom. There were openings at either end of the east and west boom to permit boats entry.

This second boom provided the favorite resting place of many birds because it offered a good view in all directions, was away from any land-based predator, and was in an area of light boat traffic.

Sometimes hundreds of ducks, gulls, and other birds would spend hours snoozing on the convenient logs. When we got too close, they would rise up and usually fly a short distance, only to circle back and land near the comfortable log.

Follow the Swallows

Early in our fishing careers, Jim and I learned that there was some merit in noting the activities of swallows. We watched the surface of the lake constantly for rises, which would tell us where the fish were and whether they were in a feeding mode.

Later, when we started to fish with flies – pretty much trolled or mooched rather than cast – we learned to row quickly to the areas where the swallows were taking insects near the surface of the lake. This paid off bigtime in smaller lakes in our area when we were dragging flies. It was also helpful when we were trolling spoons and bait or lures in American Lake. Some of the most frantic trout-catching occurred with swallows almost parting our hair as they swooped and dipped after insects.

It took me a while to figure out that swallows actually hit the water in their quest for bugs. I do not know if this is intentional or accidental, but for a while it had me fooled. It is not easy to tell from a hundred yards away if that rise on the surface is a feeding fish or a swallow with a wingtip in the water.

In addition to the other birds usually around in the summertime, we got lots of visits from gulls and mergansers. The gulls perched not only on the logbooms, but on the occasional roof or flagpole or whatever was handy along the lakeshore.

The gulls would sometimes get close enough to a boat with an anchored fisherman to beg for a handout, but they were not nearly so aggressive in this respect as the mallard ducks. Mallards have adapted to encroachment on their territory to the point where they are almost family pets. Some home owners regularly go out on their docks or sloping lawns at the lake to throw out bread scraps and even to quack as convincingly as they can. Ducks swim up to men and women and kids in boats and offer to grab up sandwich parts or salmon eggs or worms or whatever, if you care to donate.

Did We Make a Monster?

Everyone is familiar with the story of the bald eagle, our national symbol. They are beautiful big birds, but I think Ben Franklin had it right when he suggested the wild turkey be named our national bird. We all know how DDT almost wiped out the eagle and how it recovered in great style.

I never used to see eagles at American Lake to my knowledge. I say this because I wouldn't have recognized one if I had seen it, they were so rare. Today you can see eagles often and even scrutinize their nests in some of the tallest evergreens.

There is a lake 30 miles away to the southeast where I can show you a tree with an eagle nest in plain view. At American Lake they are not so visible, but they can be seen in flight and resting in tall trees.

Now, in 2010, there are reports that eagles have been killing enough birds of varied species that observers have started to worry how much of a favor we did to rescue the eagle.

Another spectacular bird sometimes seen at the lake is the osprey. This black and white bird seems like a smaller version of the bald eagle. It is a spectacular fisherman, and one of the real thrills of fishing is seeing an osprey plunge headlong into the water in quest of its prey. Unfortunately for the osprey, the eagle often acts the big bully and takes away a fish from the smaller bird. This is a good plan, because the osprey is more skilled than the eagle at fishing.

In addition to the birds named, one can see from time to time all the local avian crowd that one sees in the city: crows, jays, robins, chickadees, junkos, sparrows, finches, and all the rest. I haven't seen a kingfisher, but I would bet there is one or more somewhere along the brushy shore.

On the Bank, in the Pool

I have been saving one animal to mention to you. It is one of my favorites, something like the unicorn in that I never saw one. But maybe you did. I understand they get really big and should not be hard to see if you get the chance.

But I did hear one from time to time on the old boathouse dock. I heard it only in the middle of the night or at least when it was as dark as it gets.

The sound seemed to be coming from the southwest corner of the big dock on which my sleeping shack sat. I lay in my sleeping bag and sat up partly to hear it better. It was different from any animal sound I have ever heard. Did you ever pull a big old rusty nail out of wood after it had been there a long time? Well, when you reefed on your crowbar or claw hammer and the nail screamed its reluctance to come out after so long, that is the sound a bullfrog makes as well as I can describe it.

At the same time as the nail is being pulled, there is a hybrid undertone accompanying as if the offspring of a humming electric motor crossed with a bass fiddle was living in that nail hole.

It is a sound I would like to hear again in the still of night at American Lake with only the gentle lapping of waves against the dock for accompaniment. It is a sound created to be heard before a night of sound sleep and dreams of yellow perch swimming around your hook.

— Deaf as a Scotsman —

A truly beautiful scene gradually appeared out of the morning mist about fifty yards straight out from our dock toward Silcox Island. Many mornings were foggy and this one was no exception. On Sunday mornings like this there were thirty or more rowboats anchored in clusters in front of the boathouse.

Darkness cloaked the gathering of this fleet. The first arrivals jockeyed for what they thought might be the best positions, that is, directly over the springs in about 40 feet of water. Each boat was secured by two anchors fashioned from paint cans or coffee cans filled with cement. Grandpa had set wire loops into the concrete. These were used to tie lengths of quarter-inch rope long enough to reach the silty bottom.

When the day lightened and the fog or mist dissipated, it was often found that some anglers had missed their target and had anchored away from the desired spot. This was because the landmarks used to locate the springs were obscured from sight. So a number of fishermen laboriously pulled up their anchors and made adjustments to suit their best guesses.

Position was everything. On most mornings when the fish were biting, it was easy to see that those near the springs caught more fish than others. In fact, many anglers caught their limit of 20 fish in short order. As they pulled up their anchors and left, others moved into the hot spot they had vacated.

A Map of Sorts

In order to find the area of the springs, one lined up on four marks. The first was a particularly large Douglas fir on the slope of the boathouse, about half way down. Directly across to Silcox Island, there was a distinct pathway from the shore leading up into the woods. These two marks gave an east-west axis to the precise angler. Then, to the south at the point where the gentle slope of a cove ran out, there was a large white house with an imposing flagpole. One located the flagpole and then turned his gaze to a point jutting out from the north in a westerly direction. Where an imaginary line drawn between the flagpole and point intersected with the one drawn between the path and the large tree, this became the magic spot above the springs.

The trouble with all this was that weather and the dark of early morning made these key landmarks difficult to see. If you couldn't see them, then you just had to make as good a guess as you could.

Once you located your fishing position, you anchored and proceeded to "find bottom." This was accomplished by attaching a weight to the hook at the end of one's line. The hook and leader were fastened to the end of a line, which was usually on a rod and reel. Then the angler stripped in just enough line so that the pole bent down to touch the surface of the water. The sinker's being lifted from the bottom was easily felt through the sensitive pole. When this was accomplished, the angler knew that his bait would be just as far from the bottom of the lake as the tip of his rod was from the surface. The bottom-finding weight was removed and the hook baited, and the angler was ready for business.

One wanted to have a sensitive rod. Mine was one of the inexpensive bamboo rods my uncles had given to me and my brother and cousin Billy for Christmas. The rods were made in Japan and they came in a balsa case with a sliding top. The three-piece rods had an extra stout section for trolling and the box contained some lead weights, garish big flies, and some other gear. Most of the rods were eight to nine feet long, but some anglers used flexible shorter rods. A few, notably the Swedish family that regularly rented boats from us, fished with handlines. While the rest of us were enjoying playing the fish and feeling the tugging on our outfits, the Swedes just hoisted the little silvers over the side of the boat and figuratively into the frying pan.

A notable compromise was struck by one John Asplund, who lived near Spanaway and did some farming there. He had a casting rod that he used to hook the fish, but then he set the pole down and hauled in his catch hand over hand. When he caught a particularly small fish and was being kidded by others, he would say, "Yah, but he is big enough to stink the pan."

I was so keyed up about fishing that I sometimes snapped my leader while setting the hook. Other times, I mis-timed the upward move of my rod and the fish stripped away my bait. Setting the hook was an activity that had the serious angler poised to make a sudden move in the split-second signaled by a slight twitch of the rod tip.

Setting the Table

In order to attract the fish, there was a lot of chumming or throwing overboard feed eggs or bran or something else to pique the fishes' interest and stimulate their activity. Telltale oil slicks from fish eating the feed eggs added to the excitement.

But enough of fishing technique for now. I want to tell you about Jock and the rest of the social order of Sunday morning anglers.

There was a camaraderie among some of the regulars. Most of them saw one another only when they went fishing. And most of them were either retired, 4-F, or on their one day off a week as they earned a living working in the shipyards or at the motor base. So there was a good deal of chatter flowing in and out among the boats. Some of the men were old friends, and they passed along the usual, "Say hello to the missus."

One of the most enjoyable people was a Scotsman we called Old Jock. He was the caretaker for the cabins that Puget Sound Power and Light had built for their employees' vacation use. These cabins were set back from the wooded shore near the point with the military sign, just north of two of the little islands. I never laid eyes on the cabins themselves because they were on private property, and Jim and I had plenty of places to go without trespassing.

Fancy Seeing You

It was not unheard of that men who saw each other infrequently would suddenly recognize one another as the fog lifted on a fishing morning. So one day, when Jock took a rare morning off with a couple of friends to try to catch some fish, someone who knew him was happy to see the old fellow.

"Hello there, Jock. Hi, Jock, can you hear me?" Someone nudged the old Scot and pointed in the direction of the voice. Jock waved.

The other man yanked on his pole a little late and missed hooking the fish. He sighed and pulled in his line hand over hand to repair the bait. At the same time, he intoned, "Is your missus feeling better?" Now Jock was onto the game. Someone was talking to him in that boat over there, or that one, maybe.

"I went to church last Sunday, so help me," Jock said with a chuckle. To which the man replied, "Did your neighbor use those old boards from the barn to make his fence?" Jock smiled. "Oh, most of them are using worms and eggs, but I'm using periwinkles."

"Jesus Christ," muttered the man, "we might as well not be in the same county." From there, the conversation petered out.

The little silvers – we didn't call them kokanee until many years later – were hard fighters. In those days, many of them were only six or seven inches long, but they were as bright as a new dime and solid little fish, although their mouths were soft and they had to be played carefully. The limit in those days was 20, and many an angler caught 20 or more in his enthusiasm or greed.

Bobby Firch was a specially gifted angler. He was the crewcut blond son of the owner of the other boathouse. Bob was two or three years older than I. Of course, he had grown up fishing in the lake, and I am sure no one was better at hooking the quick little silvers and playing them into the net.

He had a summer job working at the motor base, or logistical center as it became known. Sometimes in the morning he would be anchored not far from me and always near the springs, and I could not but admire how he quickly baited his hook, threw the line over the side, rinsed the slime off his hands from his last catch while the bait descended 40 feet to a few inches off the bottom. Then he kept an eagle eye on his rod tip and when the slight twitch of a bite came, he set the hook firmly and made the rod bend as he stripped in line.

He had to get home, bolt breakfast, and make it to work at a designated time. "Seven minutes to go," he said as he glanced at his wristwatch. "And five fish to catch." Like as not he would finish his limit on schedule. No time to clean his catch. Just row like hell for the home dock, race up the ramp, put the fish in a refrigerator, wolf down breakfast, and out the door to get his ride from a friend or drive himself to work a few minutes away.

Bob went on to get his degree in fisheries at the U of Washington School of Fisheries. He was a starting forward on the Clover Park High basketball team and a kind of All-American boy. From time to time he had opportunities to razz me because I was younger and clumsy while learning to fish, but he stopped a little short most of the time, although provoked.

His dad, Old Man Firch, however, was another sort. He appeared to be at least a little odd. One time I remember his verbal assault on someone who was pegging rocks at mallards. "Cut that out or I'll run you in!" he yelled. Another time – the only time I ever saw him fishing – he hooked into something on the bottom. He was firmly into a log or root or whatever, and he got down on his hands and knees in the boat bottom to tug at his line. "I think I got a big one," he puffed.

I can attest that at times it is a little difficult to tell if you have a fish or the rest of the world on your line. But it appeared obvious even to me that time. Others remarked that the old guy could be a bit belligerent, but I feel he was just protecting his property and society from the evil ones.

I've told you some details of how we fished for silvers in the old days. Most everyone stillfished and used worms, salmon eggs, and caddis fly larva, which we called periwinkles, for bait. It was de rigeur to fish very near bottom where the feed eggs settled. We seldom fished up from bottom as much as a foot.

When the silvers bit, it was usually just a light tap or sometimes two. The tense angler had better respond to the slight sign by lifting the tip of his pole swiftly and with authority. Otherwise, the fish was gone and the bait had to be hauled in and checked to see if it were worthy of enticing another bite.

But a well-timed response would result in that feeling that all anglers know of a lively fish ready for a fight. Sometimes the fish would pull violently for the bottom or to the side, resulting in an arced rod and making one wonder if there was a whale on the other end of the line. And, of course, the fish jumped high and wide as they struggled to get free.

Big fish were rare, but they showed up from time to time. I will tell you about a few of them in a later chapter.

In the meantime, remember how Shorty taught you to thread a worm up past the eye of the hook and watch your rodtip carefully.

— They're in There! —

"They're in There!"

The fisherman was puzzled. He squinted his eyes a bit and rubbed an imaginary itch on his nose. What did the big old man who smelled like a five cent stogie mean?

The question had been, "How's fishing?" That's about as simple and clear as anyone could ask it.

"They're in there!" That was the answer spoken out of the grizzled orifice that had lately held the five cent cigar. "They're in there!"

The old man's reply gave the fisherman, or angler, something to think about. Actually, he didn't give a hoot what anyone called him. He had come to the lake on a rare day off to relax and have a nip or two from the bottle he carried in his old hunting jacket. It was good Bourbon whiskey he had saved for a rainy day and, although just a few clouds floated slowly above, this, he determined, was that rainy day.

The old man took the proffered dollar bill and gave a quarter in change. The fisherman followed as the oldster selected a pair of oars from the many leaning against the green plywood shack. The old man looped the handles of a pair of seat cushions around his wrists, picked up the oars, and led the way to a row of sturdy rowboats on the nearby shore.

Were They Really?

"They're in there!" Perhaps the old man's answer made some kind of sense after all. Still, as he stroked the oars and carefully avoided bumping the docks on either side of the aisle of water leading to the lake proper, the angler seemed to be deep in thought.

There is no need for anyone else to be puzzled or taken aback, or anything like that. The answer Grandpa Seidelman gave to the angler was his way of saying he had no idea how the hell the fishing was or would be. But one had to have a standard answer to the anticipated standard question from an excited customer. After all, there was seventy-five cents at stake here, although it was not likely a fisherman would decide to stay on shore if the answer to his question was negative.

Actually, Grandpa had two standard answers to queries about the current state of fishing. The second answer was "They're getting a few."

The beauty of these two answers goes beyond the obvious. A man does not cross an ocean as a teenager with his family, work his way across a great part of the continent enduring long six-day shifts in sawmills, nor father at least eight children without picking up some knowledge from the school of hard knocks.

If you tell someone the fishing is lousy or that the rainbow trout have a mysterious disease, there is the possibility of turning away a potential customer.

A Soft Answer

If, on the other hand, you are too enthusiastic – "Gosh, mister, I'm glad you've come out to the lake. The fish are biting like hell, and you're sure to catch a limit. The other day one fellow even had a fish jump right into his boat!" – you are running the risk of being labeled a liar, or at the best a car salesman or perhaps an evangelical preacher.

Future business must be considered as well as the immediate reward of a boat rental today.

But you don't have to worry too much about losing business. Like our early morning angler mentioned before, most people just want to get out on the water and give it a try. The average angler is convinced that he can catch as many or more and as big or bigger than you ever dreamed of catching. If he tells you anything else, he is being falsely modest.

On the other hand, if fishing is really good and just about everybody and his dog is loading up on fresh-caught trout and you get skunked, most anglers have several built-in excuses.

"That damn cheap leader" – we heard a lot of that during the war and it was true – "just snapped like a pretzel." That is one.

"I swear those fish quit biting at precisely nine oh three. We got our bait in the water at nine oh four. Up to that time, all the fellows we talked to said they knocked them over." And so forth. You get the idea.

Gramps sized up each inquiring angler before giving what seemed to be an original and spontaneous answer. No matter which answer he gave, his reputation for veracity floated high.

Can one deny that they (the fish) are in there (the lake)? That is one great thing about lake fishing. They are in there. Or they are in there if someone put them in there or they were lucky enough to find a spring or stream in which to spawn and reproduce. Of course if you get what the Game Department calls a "class failure," then school's out. But that should not happen.

Degrees of Response

Now that brings us to the second response or Plan B if you prefer: "They're getting a few." One has to be a bit more careful with that one. Truly, however, it applies to almost all waters in which men and others fish.

Rare is the day during a decent fishing season when someone is not catching a fish or two somewhere. I know guys who will stay out till well after dark trying to catch just one fish so they can say they have never been skunked.

My friend Emil Auer was such an angler. He taught several of us a simple and effective way of mooching or trolling small flies in the evening that almost always drew action from rising trout. He was a Bavarian like Grandpa, but in barely any way similar to the other old man. Emil took lots of kids and women who had never caught a trout before fishing. He liked to brag that he could teach anyone to catch a fish. "I can help a woman catch a fish. I can help a kid catch a fish. I can teach a dog to . . . ."

One night the fates were unkind and Emil got skunked. He was humiliated. He hung his Bavarian head in shame.

I told him of the many times I had not had even a bite, even though I fished hard for hours. I used to have a rule of thumb that I wouldn't even notice until I had been skunked three times in a row at American Lake. Then I screamed and perhaps went fishing at another lake.

Actually, those dry spells at American Lake were usually occasioned by the water being too cold. Once it warmed up, say about by May 1, fishing got much better. So, unless there was one of those class failures, life went on.

And Then There Are Liars

I have told you pretty much about how things stood between the inquiring fisherman and Grandfather. But we boys growing up had experience with resorts and others who rented boats at a number of lakes within driving distance. My experience with information given out by resorts and boathouses made me cautious.

The result was: I don't believe it. Even though we can give the benefit of the doubt to most everyone, it is best not to believe anything positive gleaned from boat renters over the phone. Or it was in the old days when we relied so much on the telephone to get information so easily accessible today on other electronic devices.

Renting boats was popular enough that there were times and places where it was advisable to reserve a rental. My friend Jack Berg used to get fits when he made a reservation over the phone with the resort owner at Silver Lake, an older fellow who was also named Berg. The old fellow got mixed up to the point Jack almost felt he was the one renting out the boats.

But talking to Grandfather in person could be confusing enough. Not that the old man was stupid; far from that. It was just that he looked at the world in his own way and was happy enough to have you do that too, if you were capable.

Running and Spelling

For one thing, Gramps had his own method for spelling. There was no way he had a grade school education. If he had a couple of years, that would surprise me.

So when he wrote a message on a shingle attached to a stake at the top of the hill leading down to the boathouse, the words read: "No runing down hill." Not a monumental error, but symptomatic.

Another sign read "Wearms for sale."

It never occurred to him to ask anyone how to spell anything. He spelled supplies spples, and that was no abbreviation, in the registry and account book we kept in the office. But you could bet he added up the receipts correctly and honestly.

So it was not in Gramps' nature to lie to anyone about the quality of fishing at any given time. "They're in there," said it all.

Introducing the Residents

This might be a good time to answer the question: If they are in there, who are they? Fair enough, let's try.

First and foremost among fishlife in American Lake are trout, the fish most sought after by those supposedly referred to by H. L. Mencken as the American Booblick. There are lots of spiny ray fish in the lake, too, but most people are focused on trout.

For the past many years, maybe 50, the rainbow trout is the most desirable fish likely to be caught. This is partly because this aggressive fish tends to feed all day, off and on. Rainbows also tend to strike on a wide variety of lures and baits. The more numerous kokanee, which are landlocked sockeye salmon rather than trout, usually bite well only early or late in the day. They require some refinements in technique and lures/baits that may elude many anglers.

A successful troller will often catch a mixture of these two fine fish, and many anglers can't tell the difference between them. We used to call the kokanee "silver trout" in my boathouse boy days.

You can tell the difference between a salmon and a trout by counting the divisions in the ventral fin. If they are ten or fewer, the fish is a salmon. If more, the fish is a trout. Or is it the other way around? I forget, because this is no problem to me. The streamlined kokanee, tapered at both ends, its sides gleaming with bright silver and its tail forked, is not hard to identify. And the fish has a smaller mouth with a much more delicate set of "lips" and much tinier teeth.

Back during the war days, the catch of a rainbow of any size in American Lake was exciting. I remember one time when a couple of anglers decided to anchor a bit north of the usual stillfishing spot over the springs and they caught two large rainbows. Probably those rainbows came into the lake from Murray Creek, because I doubt the Game Dept. folks planted anything except silvers.

Grandfather rhapsodized to anyone who would listen. He rattled off the weights of the two rainbows, which was something like four pounds, seven ounces and three and three-quarters pounds.

There have been many larger rainbows caught in recent years in the lake, but catches of large rainbows, including the Donaldson strain and triploid trout, have been common in many lakes in our neck of the woods in the intervening years.

Kokanee Is King

The kokanee, or landlocked sockeye salmon, is the most numerous and most desirable of American Lake fish. They are planted in the lake by the thousand as tiny little fellows. They thrive in the deep clear water of the lake if they can avoid the seagulls, mergansers, trout, bass, and other predators.

The kokanee or "silvers" feed on plankton and they live three or four years. I have caught some up to 15 inches and have talked to reputable fellows who claim to have caught some to 18 inches.

In the old days we caught them mainly by stillfishing, but trolling is the way to go today. With so much activity on the water, it is not easy to stay anchored and quiet with all sorts of boaters making the water rise and fall. Besides, almost everyone has an electric trolling motor, which makes fishing most pleasant.

The best place to catch kokanee is either on top where one may see them rising or in the correct "thermoplane" of water, where the fish finds the best temperature suited to its food supply. This is often about 30 feet down, I have found. In the old days, we tried to anchor in 40 feet of water and to fish extremely close to the bottom. This procedure became a habit.

The kokanee is a great eating fish, especially home smoked to perfection. And it is a great fighter for its size. When hooked near the surface, it jumps athletically and when it takes a bait or lure from the depths, it pulls strongly.

A Sprinkling of Cuts

Cutthroat trout are also longtime denizens of the lake. They are many fewer than rainbows but a few may be mixed in through the season in the persistent angler's catch. You are liable to run into a cutthroat anywhere in the lake, especially along the more brushy parts of the shoreline and in shallower water than some other fish.

I recall one time when two older fellows were coming in with a nice catch of decent-sized cutthroats. My younger brother and I were just about to head out to see if we could catch a fish or two. The fishermen pointed across the lake to the shoreline just to the south of the hospital buildings. It was a heavily treed and brushy shoreline with water that was shallower and that got deeper more gradually than usual.

A Tip Passed Down

"Just follow that shoreline and get in real close to the trees, boys," the oldster said. "You can work your flatfishes where it is really shallow," he continued.

Billy Paul and I rowed across the lake and followed the old man's instructions. To our delight, we caught several cutthroat up to a foot long and had numerous strikes, although we fished faster than we should have with our small flatfishes.

Larger cutthroat were sometimes taken when anglers noticed them devouring feed eggs near anchored boats. The fisherman who took off all his lead weight and patiently let his salmon eggs drift down could sometimes entice a large fish that way.

Bass and Perch

Smallmouth bass had been in the lake for many years until the Game Department killed all the fish with rotenone. Up to that time, the sporty smallmouth provided a challenging fishery. Bass fishing takes time usually, but the pugnacious bass will tackle a bait or lure larger than he is, himself, so they are catchable.

In the springtime, I used to enjoy the bass fishery immensely. The sight of a good smallmouth cruising in shallow water made my heart race.

The bass were put in the lake back in the time before 1900 when some rich guys paid to have them sent by rail from "back east." I believe all our spiny-rayed fish came in this way originally.

The yellow perch is probably the most widespread and perhaps most numerous fish in the lake. When Jim and I started to catch them through Grandpa's dock, this must have surely been the case.

At times they have been so prevalent that the lake has been filled with small perch, maybe six inches long, competing with each other for whatever they could find to eat. I believe this is called a cycle, but that may be something like a class failure. I don't know.

But I do know that today many people have realized there are fish other than trout that fight hard and are good to eat. So the perch have been thinned out some. I have caught any number of 12 and 13, even 14-inch perch over the years. On a flyrod, they will give you a tussle and do everything a trout will except jump.

Filets Are the Ticket

I never learned to filet fish, but perch and bass may be scaled and the fins and most of the spines removed so a person can eat them in a degree of comfort. Any young angler would do well to learn to filet. I know how one is supposed to do it; I just never tried to learn by doing.

The ubiquitous rock bass is everywhere in shallower water at the lake. It doesn't get big and it does not jump, but it fights extremely hard for its size and is a good fish to eat, if you contend with the spines.

In recent years, I have been amused when accounts in the local newspaper have said the rock bass are biting. Rock bass are always biting if you can get a bait or plug or lure anywhere near them.

Jim and I used to catch a lot of them mixed in with the perch under the dock. A rock bass over six inches long is a big one.

Other Residents

The lake no longer holds carp. These were poisoned out during the big killing in the 50's. I never heard of anyone catching a carp in American Lake, mainly because no one fished for them.

But that little lagoon near the old gray building was where they went to spawn, and I was privileged to see many huge carp crowded into that small area. They were kind of like a piscatorial version of college kids on spring break in Florida.

I thought about taking my trusty yewwood bow over to the spawning area to see if I could get a line onto a few of those large fish, but I thought better of it. In the first place, I didn't know if it were legal, and in the second place, I had a lot of other fish to pursue at the time, so never got around to it.

Other Fish and Fables

The lake has always had a few brown bullheads, which we call catfish and which can get pretty large. They are easy to catch when you run into them because they do not see well and will readily grab a worm dropped in front of them. Because of its cool water temperature and lack of muddy bottom, American Lake does not tempt catfish fishermen.

The state game management people have put bass back in the lake, I understand, which is interesting. And I even caught a bluegill sunfish in the lake. Whether it was put in by the state or a disgruntled angler, I don't know.

The little sculpins which live in the rocky places along the lakeshore provide a good source of food for perch and bass. They are sometimes caught by mistake by anglers and they get to be at least five inches long, although most of them are only two or three inches long.

Grandpa claims there were Loch Leven trout in the lake, and he probably is right. These are lake trout, which are really char and not trout at all. They get to be huge, maybe 20 or 30 pounds. I never heard of anyone catching a lake trout in American, but Gramps liked to tell of anglers having a lot of line stripped off their reels, only to lose their spoons and sinkers to a huge fish they never saw.

It stands to reason that the same old rich guys who paid to have bass and perch shipped in from the Middle West would have some lake trout brought in too. If so, it is likely these imports died out and were not able to reproduce in the lake.

The idea of some exotic fish, particularly big ones, added some romance to the act of fishing. After all, unlike saltwater, where one is at the mercy of tides and migrations of fish from many miles away, any fish in the lake has nowhere else to go. The largest fish in the lake may grab your lure or bait at any time.

They're in there!

Grandpa John Seidelman in his Independent Order of Odd Fellows regalia.

— The Only Way to Catch a Fish —

Once my Uncle Oscar told us of a doctor who took vacations in the same British Columbia area where Oscar, "The Lucky Dutchman," hunted for moose every year. One of the lakes in that area is Big Bar Lake, a beautiful body of water whose waters are so clear that one could see the distinct side-by-side colors that resulted from a sudden change in water depth. This drop-off marks the spot where the lake bottom apparently plunged off what amounted to an under-water cliff.

This was handy when we fished in Big Bar, because it was good fishing right along where the two colors met. So Oscar and I trolled along in our leaky rented rowboat and enjoyed some great fishing for 13 inch and 17 inch Kamloops.

Back at the lodge on an earlier trip, the doctor pontificated to other guests, including Oscar, at the lodge about fishing, among a wide range of subjects, all of which fell into the physician's areas of expertise.

"The only way to catch these Kamloops is with a flatfish," the learned one declared. Oscar and the others sipped their coffee, poked up the fire, and settled down for a boring lecture.

You see, as experienced anglers, they knew that trout – Kamloops or not – can be induced to bite on a plethora of items, some of them strange indeed.

At that very lake and earlier in the day, Uncle Oscar and his two traveling companions had caught a number of large and vigorous trout on a Carey Special fly and on some thawed shrimp Oscar pulled out of the dry ice container he always took on his trips to the north.

Setting a Trout Table

You can read all sorts of articles in hunting and fishing magazines that extoll the virtues of catching huge trout on flies so tiny you can break your eyes looking at them. According to the articles, you won't catch anything but a cold unless you tie up the size 16 or smaller hook using a microscope.

Beware of such foolishness. It is true, that tiny flies can be the undoing of big fish. But so can big juicy nightcrawlers. Sometimes it is just how hard you want to work. Some people just have to catch a trophy fish to have it stuffed so they can hang it on the wall of their den or in their office where all the other employees can see how hairy-chested the angler is. This is okay if you are really that dedicated an angler, but maybe it would be better to take a hike up that nearby hill to look for exotic birds instead. Or one can take a frozen trout out of the fridge and let it thaw for dinner. It may not stick out over both sides of the pan, but it will make a good meal nonetheless.

Fishing is surely one of the most satisfying pastimes in this life but it is still just part of life to most of us. It is not necessary to prove one's superiority by catching more or larger fish. Pleasant hours spent fishing, especially with an agreeable companion, and an occasional trout meal are goals enough.

In some respects, trout and people resemble each other. If you get hungry for lutefisk – and how could you? – and want nothing else for your meal, you are like a trout that finds an abundance of one kind of insect and can't see anything else to eat. Or maybe you like smorgasbords or buffets. A little herring here, a bit of sauerkraut and pork there, and some of that brown sugar-cured ham. You get the idea.

Unless I am starving for fish and have lost the canned tuna and can opener, my feeling about fishing is to give the fish a variety of wholesome lures and/or bait. Maybe a F-7 flatfish, yellow and red, followed by a Daredevel spoon or a Needlefish. Then go to bait if that doesn't work: half a night crawler spinning behind your spoons, or two or three maggots on the point of a hook. Maybe even a hook covered with Pautzke's soft and satisfying salmon eggs.

And if that is not good enough for them, to hell with it. Might as well leave your favorite flatfish or Triple Teezer on in hope of snagging a suicidal fish while you open up a can of beer or your thermos of coffee.

Buy Yourself a Trophy

There will be days when fish will be reluctant to bite. You might even think there are no fish in the lake. Perhaps the water is too cold or plankton have gone into "bloom" and trout cannot see your pretty little spinner.

So you have alternatives: You can go through your tackle box and tie on 73 different lures one after another. Or you can save the wasted time you used taking off and putting on different lures. This time can be spent slowly trolling around the lake with a favorite lure trailing behind as you soak up the sights. You can think about the houses or motorboats you would prefer to own as you silently cruise by. Maybe there will even be girls swimming from that dock over there. Or ducks leading their little ones in and out of the reeds near shore.

I don't need to beat this to death. You get the picture. Your sandwich and donut and warm coffee will taste wonderful in the fresh air, and who knows? You might – whoops! Look at that rod bend. I guess my old yellow and red F-7 flatfish didn't look so bad after all to one crazy fish.

Now if you feel you have to catch some trout or even a big trout before you can face the folks at home, you have other alternatives galore. You can go to a trout farm and pay a ridiculous price to catch some trout that you will pay for by the yard. Or you can stop at your favorite supermarket and buy some trout or salmon, if you can find some that does not smell fishy. Fresh fish does not smell fishy.

Or you can say to hell with it and take up golf. Or better still, order yourself a trophy from the local engravers. Make it out to yourself with your name on it and say something like "First Place in the Brook Trout Division, Lake Filakreel, July 1, 2002." Then stick it on your desk or in any other appropriate place.

Tackle and Tactics

People used to tell tales of barefoot young fellows who caught fish from local waters using a bent pin for a hook and a willow switch or cane pole with a piece of Cuttyhunk line and not a very long one at that. Undoubtedly, many of those tales are true. But you don't hear them anymore.

Just as youngsters can't play baseball without uniforms, batting gloves, cleats, and such, today's kids have to be equipped with spinning reels, graphite rods, monofilament lines, and anything else to assure their catching lots of big fish.

It is understandable that older people enjoy seeing little folks fishing and catching fish. But I wonder how much of this is Daddy wanting Junior to succeed where the old man failed. And, perhaps, a doting dad who all but assures "a limit" for his three-year-old is depriving the toddler of knowing that fishing, like life, is not always instantly successful. There is a wonderful feeling in store for the ten-year old who finally catches some desirable fish after a few years of bumbling apprenticeship.

I am getting to an axiom about fishing. It is my belief that it should be the top – and maybe the only – goal of fishing to enjoy the activity. Numbers and sizes of fish caught are mere corollaries. Maybe we should not ask how many we caught but rather whether we had a good time. And how were the sandwiches Mother made?

I have seen a father moving along in a canoe with an infant less than a year old strapped in a seat quite safely. Right near the kid, within easy reach if it had any concept of what one does when a fish strikes, was a short rod with a spinning reel clamped so that the rod bent but stayed in place when a fish struck. A small trolling spoon at the end of sixty feet or so of monofilament line was occasionally struck by a curious or hungry fish. When this happened, Junior just slept or chewed on his pacifier or peed his pants or worse.

Can't you hear Father a few years down the road? "Yes, Harley has always loved to go fishing. Why, even before he could walk, I took him out in the canoe and he loved to watch his pole bend when they hit that little Triple Teezer. Now he likes to fish for tuna and sailfish and wonders when they will open the season on whales."

A Hunk of Cutty?

It is often true that one can catch fish with the cheapest and simplest tackle. Safety pins and willow switches may be stretching it a bit, but the stuff Jim and I used at the lake in the old days was not much to cause bragging.

I mentioned the inexpensive Japanese bamboo rods our uncles had given us for Christmas. Jim had a telescoping metal rod that was a doozy for carrying on the bus and which served well enough for both stillfishing and trolling in our young world.

The reels brother Paul and Cousin Billy and I got for Christmas were shaped like casting reels but you couldn't cast with them. As Uncle Oscar said, they were good for reeling in and storing the line between fishing trips.

And the line on those reels was a black and white braided and enameled line called flyline. You couldn't really cast flies with it, but it was okay for stillfishing. Better than Cuttyhunk. Never heard of Cuttyhunk? Well, you are lucky you never had to fish with it. It was a sturdy green cloth line that went completely limp in the water and made the most complex snarls you could imagine.

Cuttyhunk was ideal for fishing without a pole and/or reel. You could manipulate it without fear of cutting your hands, and it was strong enough to hold a salmon if you ever fished in salt water and got that lucky. The Swedes who rented boats from us and who hand-fished for silvers in American Lake probably used Cuttyhunk.

Of course, I didn't know better, but I had heard of flyfishing along with some of the usual propaganda that put this method of fishing on an imaginary pedestal. So I tried to tie my own flies with big hooks and feathers obtained here and there. By Golly, I wanted to go after the fish one read about in Field & Stream or other outdoors magazines.

It might give you a laugh to picture me at age 14, standing on the corner of the big dock at Don's Boathouse and casting – if I can use that term – in the direction of the smaller dock a few feet away. The wet line hung like one string of very flexible spaghetti as I whipped my bamboo rod and tried to will the clinging line through the guides. But it was obviously futile from the first, and I soon caught on and abandoned flyfishing for a while.

An All-Purpose Bait

The angle worm is an angler's best friend. And not just a beginner at that. If you had to pick one bait or lure to the exclusion of all others, you would do well to head for the garden and the leaf pile. Worms will take trout of all kinds, perch, bass, catfish – just about any kind of fish you can name. They may be fished in any number of ways: below a bobber, cast and retrieved carefully so they won't break apart, stillfished deep, and trolled plain or behind spoons or as a garnish in small pieces on hooks of lures such as flatfish. If you get a worm in the water on a hook anywhere near a fish, there is likely to be a bite or at least a close encounter. Even in saltwater.

Some of the snooty people who think they are superior for fishing with dry flies only make fun of bait fishermen. And it is true that it is great fun to fish with flies. It is actually easier to catch fish on flies than with baits and lures. But there is no need to feel superior, either way.

So you can bet that Jim and I gave the worms a workout when we fished in our hole through the dock. At first, I was a squeamish kid who had difficulty in even touching an earthworm, but I soon got over that. When the perch and rockbass began to grab our baits, I got so excited I had to rush up and visit the privy on the hillside. And I raced back to the dock as soon as I could so that Jim wouldn't catch more fish than I.

Jim and I had a competitive thing going at first, but I am glad to say I was able to let it go early on. Jim was still competitive just before he died on an operating table when he was in his 80s.

He wanted to play baseball with our fishing activities. "If you get a nibble, that's a base on balls. A hard bite is a base hit, and you get a run if you catch a fish," he said. Or something like that. He probably beat me soundly and maybe that is why I decided that fishing should not be a competitive activity.

This goes double for derbies and professional fishermen. What goes on in these activities isn't fishing at all, in my opinion.

We should be teaching youngsters to enjoy going fishing, to learn about all the facets of this fascinating activity, and to appreciate the out of doors, the animals and birds as well as the fish, the camaraderie of anglers, and the quiet times to be alone and think and relax.

Is That You, Rudy?

As our society gets more competitive, we tend to breed youngsters who are rude. They are only a small percentage, but they tend to ruin things for others. Many, but not all, waterskiers fit nicely into this category.

One day on American Lake, as I trolled with my electric motor, I noticed another boat nearby. A kid of maybe ten was fishing in a big motorboat with an older person. As the kid ate his lunch, he threw his sandwich wrappings into the water. The older person ignored this. Of course, I wanted to knock the crap out of both of them, but instead just netted the floating debris for later disposal. If you say anything in a case like this, you are liable to be attacked, verbally or otherwise.

Another time I was struggling to load my boat into my pickup after a morning's fishing. A chubby twelve-year-old nearly poked me in the eye with his pole as he caught small sculpins that lived in the cover provided by the cement partitions of the launching pad. The kid continued to catch little fish while I tried to avoid getting my eye poked.

It never occurred to him or to his nearby dad that one of them might offer to help the frail old man lift his boat into the truckbed.

These incidents are not rare, but there are many more anglers who are glad to help others. Sometimes I have spent good fishing time towing someone back to the boathouse when they have had trouble with an outboard. Invariably, these grateful boaters offer to pay, and invariably I and others turn them down. "Give someone else a tow sometime," is the general response.

I'll preach some more about boaters later, but for now just say that I am grateful for those dads and others who try to teach the young ones something like manners on the water and off. At times it seems like these people are going extinct.

How about just trying to enjoy fishing for itself? Sure, it is okay to take pride in being smarter than a fish you've caught, or in owning the biggest boat or the best depth-finder. But when you get right down to it, what is there to brag about? A professional bass angler might win a lot of money, or you could win first prize at the annual Elks salmon derby. But you'll more likely be assured of getting relaxation and peace of mind if you take it easy and try not to be superior to the other dumb sucker in the next boat.

Blessings on You, Little Man

We've come a long way from the kid with the willow switch. In some respects, this is fine. But I can't help being grateful that I knew a childhood when fishing was something you could enjoy in peace and relative quiet on a beautiful lake worthy of love and respect.

— Dragging the Gear —

To troll or not to troll. That is the question. For a gentleman named Frank Lee, the answer was a positive. Mr. Lee always rented boat No. 3, round-bottomed and double-ended, that was tethered to the protected side of the smaller of our two docks, just about where Butch was most apt to plunge into the lake in pursuit of the mocking mallard ducks.

There was another similar boat right next to No. 3, and I do not remember its number, but it was most likely No. 1 or No. 2, given Grandpa's system of numbering boats.

The stack of plywood boats atop one another on the smaller dock all had numbers in the 40s or 50s – I think 57 was the highest. Our other, more substantial rowboats along the shoreline had lower numbers in the 20s, 30s, 40s, and tens. It was a little like a football team with jersey numbers: The heavier boats had running back and linemen numbers and the double-enders were star backs. But all this didn't occur to Grandpa. They were all just boats requiring caulking, painting, and draining when it rained.

As I got the seat cushion and oars for Mr. Lee, I didn't think much of why he was different from 95 per cent of our other boat renters – the ones who, if they fished at all, needed anchors to hold them in one place.

That would have disheartened Mr. Lee. He was a troller, and all I knew was that he would energetically ply the oars until he became very small in the direction of the south end of the Vets' hospital or disappeared around the west side of Silcox Island. I knew he fished while moving and used something called spoons or gear or Pop Gear after a manufacturer of the same name who put together strings of shiny chromed spoons that spun around on their wire backbones in a manner designed to attract fish.

A Glint of Treasure

Perhaps I would never have started trolling at all except for a fortunate find. One day one of my many rowing journeys and a burst of sunshine through a gap in the clouds coincided. There, in six or eight feet of water just short of the military sign and at the margin of the sunken island was a gleam I could not ignore.

I leaned over the side of the boat and could hardly believe my eyes. There, gently fluttering in the mild current, was a set of silvery spoons – as plain as day. The spoons and the lure tied on behind them had fastened onto a log in the deceptively shallow water. I quickly put into shore a few feet away and cut a long branch from the plentiful supply of saplings that choked the shoreline.

The branch I cut had to be long enough so that with my arms extended to the fullest, I could reach the beckoning treasure. And it had to have a suitable fork to it so that I could snare the prize and pull it up. Soon I was in possession of my new tackle, and I gave it more than a once-over. It consisted of five spoons on a series of short wires connected by machine-tied loops. There were some red glass beads at strategic places and a metal rudder that kept the spoons from twisting the line. On a thick leader – it must have been 10 pounds or more – there was a large red and white lure with a triple hook called a Daredevel – I think that is how it is spelled – that became familiar to me in later years as I used smaller sizes behind my spoons, or alone, as an effective fish killer.

Unless one knows of the sunken island, it is easy to run afoul of such a setup. The angler putts along following the shoreline rather closely, where he has caught fish and had strikes before. All is well. Steam arises from his coffee as he sets it down on the seat beside him between oar strokes. The homemade cookies his wife Mabel packed for him are in jeopardy of being dunked and/or chomped when suddenly – his pole bends and lurches toward the stern of his rowboat.

A Monster Escapes

The fisherman knocks over his coffee cup in his desperate move to save his pole from a watery grave and, suddenly, as the thick but old line mercifully parts, the pole rattles limply with the reel end perilously close to the brink. Whew!

Did you see that strike? Did you see that pole bend when that big old trout hit it with full force? Took my whole outfit, dammit.

There is a brief period of mourning for the lost gear: yard-and-a-halfs, as they are called, have always been expensive, and the lure itself was not cheap, but at least the pole was saved.

Back at the boathouse, the tale is told – but not the location – by the angler. That spot might be worth trying another time after replacing that expensive set of spoons. No need to tell anyone just where that lunker lurks.

So I was now the possessor of a sparkling set of spoons: no rust, just chrome everywhere. The big Daredevel went into my rapidly filling tackle box, probably never to be used again.

However, now I was equipped to try trolling, if I so desired. And one day I did with positive results.

Lucky Louis

I don't remember who was rowing the boat. Probably Billy Paul, my little brother. I say that because I know it wasn't Jim and can't imagine who else it could have been.

Jim was fishing on the dock at the time and he was standing near the edge toward the center north and south. He let loose with a good-natured barrage of teasing when I pulled in my first ever fish caught by trolling.

You should have seen my rod. It was a stout – and I mean stout – length of bamboo, maybe six feet long. At one end it was at least an inch in diameter and at the "sensitive" end, it was about the size of a man's index finger. In other words, a fish would play hell bending that stout rod unless it weighed at least five pounds. My silver was maybe 11 inches long and it must have been under the dock near Jim's feet, because it grabbed the worm on my hook just a few feet from the dock as we started out.

"Lucky! You lucky guy!" As if the munching of a juicy worm by that fish were a Biblical miracle. I was pretty contented, although I did not get much sport out of horsing in that first silvery prize.

Time for a Change

In the next few years Jim and I began to mix serious trolling efforts with our other fishing. Eventually, as I got much older, I preferred to move around while fishing. I thought of Mr. Lee and how far ahead of the rest of us he was.

The many advantages of trolling finally sunk into my dense skull. For one thing, the seat got hard after a few hours of sitting at attention waiting for that telltale twitch of a flyrod end. When one trolled, a strike on a rod pointed perpendicular from the boat's path was readily discernible.

By then, too, a respectable fishing rod had replaced my bamboo telephone pole. Perhaps before we go further, I should explain why I dared to fish with such a monstrosity.

As I have mentioned, the years of the Great Depression were not that far behind us. We learned in those times to make do with whatever we had or could scrounge up. My bamboo pole was just one example of necessary thrift. I had managed to purchase a galvanized reel seat and some ceramic and steel eyes for the pole. The reel seat was easily taped on and the guides or eyes were glued and wrapped with Cuttyhunk line. The whole effect was something that was crude but would work within serious limitations.

Evolution in Angling

It took many years before I learned to troll effectively. For one thing, Jim and I usually rowed much too fast. The poor fish had to race to catch up with our disappearing bait. In American Lake, in particular, you want to troll mainly at a leisurely pace. I found that leaning on the oars every so often to allow my spoons to sink a few feet was a good idea. One should not abandon a brisk pace entirely, however. A general rule would be to fish generally at a slow speed, stopping completely from time to time, and then varying speed from pretty fast on down just to see how the trout are approaching lunch that day.

Also, Jim and I had somewhere got the impression that it was best to follow the shoreline fairly closely when fishing for trout. This deprived us of a lot of good fishing area way out there in the middle by the island or in front of the hospital. As far as shorelines and fish go, they are both where you find them, and they do not have a mathematical relationship, so far as I can see. Many of the biggest trout I have caught have been in the upper reaches of deep water. That is to say, fishing where it is 90 feet deep but your lure or bait is moving enticingly at about 30 feet.

Rigging up for Success

If you are going to troll spoons for kokanee and rainbows in my favorite lake, you will need a stout pole. Not so stout as my bamboo chunk of youthful days, but with enough backbone to handle a fish of considerable size. I can't give you a number or a weight but you will know when you get the right combination.

Actually, you should have two rods rigged up and at your disposal. One of these is for fishing deep and the other for trolling near the surface of the lake. You will need the heavier outfit if you want to troll deeper than 30 feet. Often, the fish in American Lake congregate or do business at 55 feet or even deeper.

To get deep enough to shake hands with the fish, you will need a substantial reel and line on your stouter pole. I resisted reeling in fish for a long time – remembering my early training courtesy of Uncle Oscar – but found it was necessary in trolling American Lake. Besides, that 13 or 14 inch trout or kokanee on your hook will fight hard enough when it grabs onto your leaded line, even with an ounce and a half sinker added.

You might think a leaded line is too much, but it is not. There are two weights of leadcore line and you will want to use the lighter of the two. A nice thing about leaded line is that it is color coded. Every 30 feet, the color changes, so you know how much line you are trailing without straining your brain. At American Lake, you will be using two or three colors most of the time.

More about Tackle

Care should be taken when rigging up to assemble an outfit that will hold the fish and make it as easy as possible for you to net your catch. It is advisable to rig up your deep-fishing outfit beforehand, say in your driveway or on your front lawn. You need to know that you can reach far enough to net a fish with your long-handled net. In case you are wondering how to get one of these useful devices, you firmly fasten a short-handled net to a section of old mop or broom pole.

Swivels are an important part of your outfit. You will discover where to place them and how sturdy they need to be. I can't give you numbers or a diagram, but I can suggest that if you err, make your mistake on the sturdy side. You don't want to lose your entire outfit because of a weak swivel.

How Deep Is Deep Enough?

You can often fish with your leaded line without an added sinker. If I use a sinker, I like to go no further than a one and one-half ounce keel sinker at the most. By arranging your line with two interlocking swivels, you can quickly add or subtract a sinker without undue loss of time.

Remember when trolling that if you stop your motion, your outfit will sink to as far down as the amount of line you are trailing. This means that if you have 30 feet of line out and you stop to let your outfit sink, it will get down 30 feet by the time it is more or less vertical. And you will be surprised how often you get strikes and catch fish when you are in this position: straight up and down. Of course, you will want to know how far the water extends under your boat, but you are safe in American Lake at 60 feet in most of the good trolling areas.

A Few Good Places

And where are these good trolling areas? Well, try the area to the north of Silcox Island. Get out far enough to avoid the under-water plateau 40 feet down and fish where it is 60 to 80 feet deep. Facing the hospital, you will see a large point of land slightly off to your right and aiming right at you. Go in that direction and make a fairly sharp turn every so often. You can fish in a roughly triangular pattern this way and you'll remain in a good trolling area. The area closer to the island is fine, too, provided you avoid dragging bottom.

At all times, notice where the other guys are fishing and whether they have their landing nets out from time to time.

Another good area most of the time is the large inlet just to the south of the officers' beach. I like to fish this area from east to west, lining up on the landing at the National Guard area and a distinctive path on the west side of the cove, which is sometimes known as "The Culvert."

Set a Trout Table

All of your preparation will go to waste unless you have something on the end of your line that will entice strikes. We have already mentioned gang trolls or yard-and-a-halfs. These are certified fish killers, but you may want something a tad lighter pulling on your line.

The dodger (originally herring dodger?) is great both for kokanee and trout. The smaller sizes, 0 and 00 are suitable. They snap onto your line with swivels and are easily changed.

I need to tell you here that you need a relatively short section of strong (10 lb, at least) leader fastened to the leaded line on one end and your spoons or dodger on the other. You can manipulate the length of this section of sturdy monofilament when you are rigging up your outfit in your driveway or on your lawn.

Now you are ready for the piece de resistance on your trout menu. There are numerous lures and baits that will do the job. Anglers argue for hours about the merits of their favorite lures.

The lure or bait, of course, goes on a leader behind your spoons or dodger. The length of this leader varies and again engenders arguments. I like to use 16 inches as a touchstone, but one may want to extend to as much as three feet of six-pound test, or three-pound if you like to live dangerously.

Watch the Wiggle

I remember my discussion one day with two Game Department agents as they carried out their duties near the south shore of Silcox Island and I pursued kokanee nearby. We compared tackle and methods of fishing and found unanimity except for the length of leader. We even agreed on the best lure at the time, which was something called a needlefish.

They favored a longer leader, say 30 inches, while I preferred one of maybe 20. "Of course," said one of the officers, "you will get more action with the shorter leader." Whatever works.

A shorter leader is perhaps better with slower speeds. It is not advisable in American Lake to fish too fast. Little bursts of speed aside, a snail's pace can pay off.

Other lures besides the needlefish that I have found good are the Triple Teezer, variations of the Daredevel, F-6 and F-7 flatfish of varying colors – I prefer orange or yellow in the main. It is good to remember that these lures can be fished with or without added bait – a tiny piece of worm or maggots or power bait.

Speaking of maggots, they are not offensive when purchased as bait and they are about as effective as you can get. The trouble with them is they are hard to get onto a hook without ruining them. I put them on a piece of styrofoam and stab the hook through rather than trying to hold them like an angle worm.

And, importantly, the liquids sold to spray on your bait or to dip your bait in are worth the price. I make my own: commercial stuff mixed with cod liver oil and anise. Dip your maggot or worm in such stuff and you will be gratified at the results.

So now that you have plenty of information to confuse you, go ahead and rig up for deep water fishing.

Switching for Success

One more suggestion. Rig up that second pole, complete with lure, and have it ready near you. You can use a lighter rod for this one, even a flyrod if you wish. I use an Eagle Claw Denco Super II 7-foot rod that is just the right weight for the purpose.

On the simplest single-action reel I can find, there needs to be a good length of heavy monofilament line. Mine is probably 20 lb test or something like that. This weight of line is needed because I strip the line with this rig, and my fingers do not get cut by the larger-diameter line while stripping in.

When I see fish working the surface, I reel in my deep rig and pick up the other one. That way I do not have to take off any weight I am using. Just switch rods, put on any bait I choose and I am in business.

You're on Your Own

There is not enough paper to be able to tell you everything about trolling, but it sure is a fine way to fish. You can enjoy your surroundings and explore every part of our delightful lake. As you fish, you will make adjustments to your tackle and you will find your own favorite lures and baits. Talk to other fishermen and exchange information with them.

Oh, to be on American Lake early on a mid-May morning with two poles rigged up and two colors of line out and a dodger followed by a two-hook leader baited with maggots doused with anise-scented oil. You will need to have a long-handled net ready nearby.

The electric motor moves along, responding to controls. Every so often you pause and let your spoons sink. You turn sharply often and fish in figure 8s or circles. Your speed varies as you cut the motor speed and then turn it up again, but not too fast.

Hold your breath. Don't knock over your coffee when that hard strike bends your pole.

Could you be any happier?

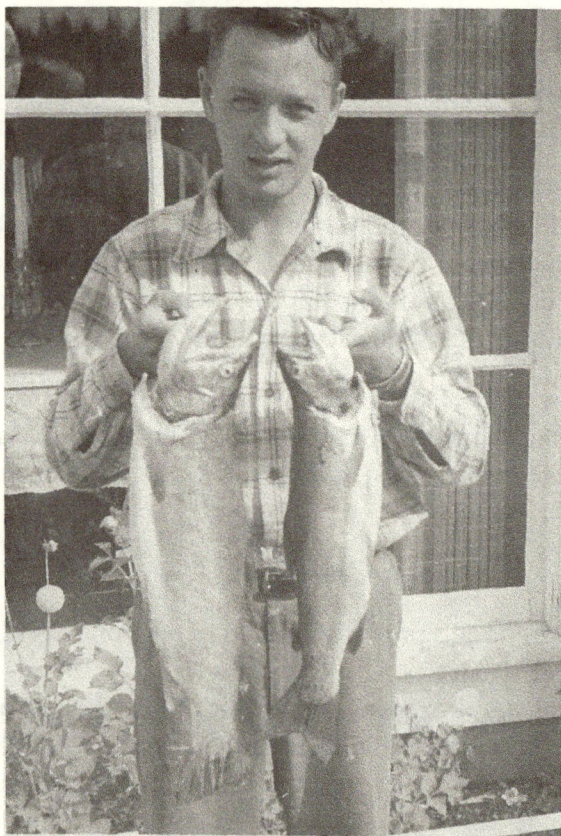

**Louis with the two large trout he caught from
Gravelly Lake while fishing with Homer Post.**

— Sit Still and Fish —

Well, class, this is what you have been waiting for. Have you brought your poles and reels and tackle box? You don't have to rig up yet. Let's talk a little first about the subject. I see a hand back there. You have a question? No, there is no prerequisite to this class unless having a lot of time to waste – er, spend, could be considered one.

First of all, this is a very old form of fishing, primitive, that is. When some fellow came out of a cave and first tried to fish with a vine for a line and a bone hook, he didn't look to climb into a cabin cruiser and put the motor into slow motion so he could drag a chunk of mammoth meat slowly behind. Those things were not invented yet. You, with the hand in the air? No, not even the Mossy Log One Sitter that is the first fishing boat found beneath tons of sediment in a dry lake in Switzerland. Take my word for it, the first sucker to crawl out of the cave hungry for stuffed sole never heard of Orvis or Cabela's or Mickey Sherman's Tackle Shop.

Keep it Simple

They had to do with what was at hand: bones, sinews, vines, rocks, stuff like that. And it was not easy at first. But in a few million years or less, they developed a way to still fish.

That is what it is called: stillfishing. We once had a student from Kentucky who thought it had something to do with fishing for stills. Boy, did that sucker have a lot to learn!

Now before I get the usual question from some infiltrator from a civil rights organization, let me answer your unasked question. Yes, this method of fishing was once known as N----- fishing. I said it only once and will not repeat it. However, in the early history of our country and perhaps back to the other side in the days of the Compleat Angler, that's what the man in the street or on the bank or in the boat called it.

"Caught seven nice trout up by the old sawmill." "How big?" "Nice ones (holding out hands wide apart) about this size." "N----- fishing or trolling?" So on and on. Well, we do not use that terminology anymore. It is unfair, inaccurate, dirty, and verboten. If you want to talk that way, take your cigar box full of clumsy tackle you bought on sale at K Mart and . . . .

Well, as I was saying, this is a most elemental way of fishing and it doesn't require any great intellectual expenditure. Nor monetary for that matter. That is a great thing about this way to fish if you are a bit short of moohlah, which begs the question of how you got into this institution in the first place.

My first tackle box was a cigar box left over after Grandfather Seidelman had smoked an entire box of Rum Crooks without apparent fatal effects. This box held, early on, a few assorted hooks picked up here and there, including a gift or two from my cousin Emmet, a red-hot fisherman who solemnly displayed his superior tackle and showed the difference between the little gold hooks and their dark-colored brethren. Emmet swore the gold hooks were far better than the others. He had actually caught several trout, and he should have known.

Also in the cigar box was some leader. Where I got it, I don't know, nor do I know where it had been. I do know it was cheap and it was brittle – not a good quality. You could snap a four-pound test piece without cutting your hands even a little bit.

There were some lead sinkers, probably all split shot of differing sizes. These had been used, but careful application of a knife blade to the squirming shot could restore vitality unless one cut all the way through and then said a forbidden word or two.

A Rod for Comfort

What else was in that box, I don't recall, but it stunk to high heavens from the cheap stogies it had held. Any fish biting near anything from that box had to have an olfactory disorder or at least a beastly cold. After I raided that old tackle box of Dittemore's, the contents of my cigar box took on an air of sophistication with any number of useless items taking up space. Reeling the time machine into fast-forward, I need several large Sears tackle boxes now, and that is just for my bass and trout lures.

Those of you lucky or rich enough to own a rod should cherish that implement. It is what sets most of us apart from the most primitive angler with his handline and hopes. It is not nice to laugh at these handline folks. They are either too impecunious or too ignorant to own a nice rod like my Phillipson Pacemaker that Uncle Oscar got for me for $26 in 1945 from a friend named Bill McQueen, who owned a little tackle shop up by the Community Theater at South 56th and M Streets, just where the bus turns to go to South Tacoma.

Well, to make this shorter – did I hear a muffled laugh? or was it a sigh? – stillfishing is great fun when you can do it. It is so simple that one laughs at fumbling citizens who knit their brows and try to make it seem complicated.

Cherchez Le Poisson

First, you need a place to fish. We have that: American Lake, and it has plenty of fish. Truly, they're in there. The problem is to get them out of there.

Now that that is settled, let's say for sake of argument that we have a boat rented and are ready to go. The question becomes, go where? So we select a well-known stillfishing place, say over in front of the Vets' Hospital. You row, I will ride shotgun in the back and complain.

So here we are. Line up on that fence running east and west on the hospital grounds. Then to the north and south, locate your rowboat roughly on an imaginary line running from the obvious point to your right as you face the shore and the not-so-obvious point to your left near the officers' beach. If you don't know these land-marks, you can go to Hell, because this is hard enough to explain already without teaching you geography as well.

Now anchor your craft. This is accomplished by lowering, hand over hand, the cement anchors provided by the thoughtful boat owner. A quarter-inch line at least 60 feet long is required for this purpose. It is considered bad form to throw the anchors into the lake. Slide them silently to the bottom, please.

The anchor ropes should go as straight down as possible and they must be tied securely to the gunwale or some such nautical thing with the right amount of play – that is to say, practically none at all – to keep your boat in one place only.

Now rig up your pole with your line and attach a leader of no more than three-pound test with properly tied hook or hooks of size ten or nine. After finding bottom (see procedure in my text Shorty Says), you are ready to bait up. Question? Yes, you may purchase the book – and it is really an excellent one – at the bookstore.

Bait your hook or hooks and toss them out a few feet toward the direction in which you will be fishing. The reason you will toss instead of cast is that you should, after finding bottom, lay your rod down and pull in the line hand over hand.

When you bait, you are at a critical stage. The bait can often make all the difference in the world. If you use a worm sandwich, remember what Shorty said. Yes? Buy the book, won't you. It won't hurt you to shell out a little.

As I was saying, the worm sandwich or even salmon eggs alone are rather old-fashioned, but Jim and I used them effectively. Then we went though the periwinkle stage. That was important to our development. No one would give us credit today, but we just about revolutionized the fishing at American Lake.

By Any Other Name

The periwinkle may not be one at all. That is to say there is a saltwater snail that sounds from the Webster definition to be a very similar thing, but our periwinkles were strictly freshwater denizens. You can find them in profusion in such streams as the Deschutes River in Thurston County or the Mashel or just about any little brook. They may also be found along the shore at shallow depths in cooler lakes like American.

Grandpa called them penny winkles, and he may have been right, although I doubt it. But for sure, they are caddis fly larva, and they are good bait at times.

I say at times, because for twenty years or so, I have not had good luck with them. In my last years of fishing, I rarely even tried them. But once they were a magic bait.

Jim and I tried some fat yellow winkles in our usual stillfishing spot in front of the boathouse. Suddenly we startled all the old-timers by pulling in more silvers than anyone else – by far. The fish just wouldn't leave our bait alone, which was fine by us.

Pretty soon Grandpa was selling periwinkles at the boathouse for thirty-five cents a dozen, same as little bait fish.

Jump into the Deschutes River. Probe the depths with your eyes. Do you see little rocks crawling around? If so, these are likely periwinkles. They are little wormlike creatures with black heads and armlike feelers. They crawl about on the bottom lugging their houses with them like turtles. These houses or cases are built by the creature much as a spider spins its web, only wetter. They will pull in their heads when they sense your presence but by then you have them in a container and on the trout menu.

Periwinkles are a little delicate. They need cool. They are okay in and out of water. Some guys put them in gunny sacks under a dripping outside faucet. Others of us put a jar in the fridge, after obtaining permission from you know whom.

Peel off the rock case. It is a little like aging rubber. This will expose the fat little white or yellow creature inside. Put the point of a hook where an Adam's apple should be and thread this killer bait onto your hook.

After you bait your hook, throw it over and watch your line sink as it heads for the bottom. Oh, I should have mentioned you will need a split shot or two – bb size – on your leader. And the leader can be a yard long but not too short. The line and leader are securely tied together as best you can.

The reason you watch the line sink is that sometimes eager fish grab your bait long before it gets to the bottom. You can tell by the rate of descent whether this is happening.

Sometimes a happy fish will swim around with your bait in its mouth for a while as you sit there like a dummy wondering if gravity has deserted you that day. And, if you have been unwatchful, you might get a hell of a bite all at once that makes you sit up straight on your boat cushion.

Barring such an early bite, locate your bait as far off bottom as you want and either hold onto your rod or place it in such a way that it rests across the gunwale and has the reel end propped on a tackle box or old boot or something, but with your hand always in contact and line secured to prevent premature paying out.

Then you can throw over some feed eggs. American Lake, because of its size, is one of the few lakes hereabouts that allow chumming.

Touches and Torpedos

Now watch your pole tip. A flyrod is almost essential for kokanee fishing this way because you need a sensitive tip. The bites are often just touches. Sometimes one touch is all you get. More often there is a second or third bump.

When that nibble comes, whip your flyrod tip upward to set the hook and be sure your reel is secured so that line does not pay out unexpectedly on you. Then enjoy the fight with the spunky trout or landlocked sockeye on your line.

Sometimes the strongest bites you get are unproductive but they are thrilling anyway. A rod may suddenly snap downward and you may feel it is a lunker for sure. But more likely it is a determined smaller fish bent on suicide or a piscatorial equivalent thereof. These kamikaze rushes sometimes break leaders or rip the bait out of the mouth of the perpetrator.

Your Guess Is as Good

I mentioned that for the past umpteen years the kokanee have turned up their snouts at periwinkles. Why? Who knows? This is something I have noticed about fish. The fool doctor who knew only one way to catch a fish might be surprised to come back 20 or 50 years later and find he couldn't buy a strike with his flatfish. Not likely, but not impossible either.

Could it just be a matter of evolution or breeding or whatever the fishy equivalent of advertising is? But it is a definite thing – the changing appetites of fish.

Therefore, it behooves one to ask the locals what they are using with the most success. They will probably lie to you, but you may provide them with some humor by asking.

Hands and Fish

You can forget a lot of what I have told you if you need or want to fish with a handline. Adapt anything I told you, but the handline method has a charm of its own. The feel of the fish on the line is exciting, and the angler can easily pay line in or out while keeping it taut. Jigging a bait up and down can also be productive. This is simulated when fishing with a pole by slowly paying the line in, inch by inch, or by jiggling the pole up and down in a more pronounced manner.

Now, I think I have told you enough about stillfishing. Get out there with the minority non-trollers and do your own version.

Oh, there is the matter of a long-handled landing net. Don't go out without one. Many a kokanee or trout has been lost because it was just out of reach of the little net like Rock Hudson carried in that movie where he was supposed to be fishing.

— Jimmy's Left-handed Day —

It was on a day when the water and the weather were just right that Jim and I made one of our many attacks on the trout population. There were only a few clouds, the breeze was light, and Mother Nature smiled on us.

So we rowed up to the point near the Soldiers' Beach that guarded the entrance to the large cove sometimes called The Culvert. We had opted to row and then row some more a fair distance to get away from the crowd of boats anchored in front of the boathouse.

Although we enjoyed talking to some of the other fishermen sometimes, some of them would just as soon not stoop to chatting with a couple of young punks. That is, until we started to catch fish. Then came a few friendly queries about what bait we were using or some other aspect of stillfishing.

We anchored that day near the Soldiers' Beach, partly for a break from potential rudeness. Anyway, we often tried places other than in front of the boathouse just to see if we could find another good spot for catching fish.

Yo, Heave Ho

In order to get to the Soldiers' Beach, one is required to pull on the oars at least 400 times. I know this, because I used to count the strokes as I rowed to fishing destinations. When you know how far it is and the time and effort required, sometimes it is a better idea to anchor with the crowd in the usual spot.

That day when we decided on the Soldiers' Beach area as our destination, we were pretty confident we would catch fish, because it was one of those times when it seemed the fish were biting everywhere.

Jim thought the fishing would be good because he had consulted something called John Alden Knight's Solunar Tables, and that worthy publication had predicted good fishing.

I don't know all the details, because I do not believe in astrology nor Buddhism, nor a lot of other stuff, including the Solunar Tables. But Jim did. In theory, the day was sometimes punctuated with short periods of time when the fish would feed, more or less vigorously. These were called major and minor feeding periods.

"We are entering a major feeding period," Jim solemnly informed the world. Since we had discussed the Knight Tables thoroughly while waiting for the bus in front of the Northern Pacific Bank the day before, there was no need for me to repeat my views.

Dinner Is Served

But there was no denying how eager those trout were. Maybe there is something more to the tables than I thought. There, the first fish of the day was nosing my bait and I had set the hook firmly. It was going to be a red letter day.

The fish came in quickly. I rinsed my hands, dried them on an old but clean rag, baited anew and tossed my bait out away from the boat. I couldn't help thinking that it was nice I could fling it as far as I wanted without landing near someone else.

Soon a trend was developing. Jim got a bite and reefed on his pole. "Missed it clean!," my friend said as he handlined his bait toward the boat so he could check his bait for worthiness.

Missing hooking a fish while stillfishing has a large component of luck in it. Simply put, it is often just a matter of which way the hook is turned. If it is toward the fish, most likely you will feel a solid response as your line tightens. If it is away from the fish, you can let your bait sit a while longer or pull it in to repair any damage and start again.

Jim's hook seemed to be turned the wrong way often that morning, while mine seemed destined to find a solid connection almost every time a fish knocked.

Soon I had five or six fish in the boat and Jim had none yet. We both felt this would change soon, but then things got worse.

I am sure I mentioned earlier that Jim had a palsy of sorts. I first became aware of this when we were eating lunch in the school cafeteria during junior high years. A good friend who had known Jim longer than I could not resist teasing him a little because he was having a time eating a bowl of soup. Seems most of the soup would dribble out bowlward as Jim's hand shook. He took this kidding with good nature, which was just like him.

But shaky hands are no help when tying a hook onto a leader. And Jim managed early on to snap a leader when he struck a little too vigorously in response to a bite. That meant tying a new hook on the leader with shaking hands.

Various other evils befell him. He snarled his line and had to take valuable time with his trembling fingers to straighten out the mess. There are few things more aggravating than having to work on a snarl while the fishing is hot. We also managed to knock a fish off as we tried to net it. Another fish spat out the bait after much swirling and jumping. I was getting many more bites than he was.

Let's Switch Seats

As I neared my limit of 20 silvers, it became problematical that Jim would ever get to that goal. We liked to catch as many as the law allowed. The limit was 20 fish each, but it was understood that if one person got to the limit and the other was not quite there, the first person could catch part of the second person's number, rather than sit and twiddle.

I got bite after bite as Jim drew but a few nibbles. It was obvious that I would have my 20 pretty soon, so I tried to slow down. When I got a good bite, I would hook the fish and then rest my rod over the gunwale and let the fish run so it would have a good chance to toss the hook. Alas, the fish stayed with me with regularity.

So I suggested switching seats. Jim then fished right where I had been. I caught another fish. So after awhile, I suggested we trade outfits. I handed him my rod. I caught another fish with his tackle. This was getting monotonous.

But I have yet to mention the crowning indignity heaped on Jim, who was probably about as fine and moral person as you could find in the old U.S. of A. That occurred when, having broken a leader when a fish wrapped it around our anchor ropes, Jim shakily selected a new leader, baited it and threw it over the side. He sat there and stared at the worm pieces and salmon eggs as they sank to the bottom.

Migod! He had neglected to tie the new leader to his line, so it descended merrily to the bottom all on its own.

After trading seats and outfits without success, we more or less gave up. At first I had kidded Jim a bit. It was the soup thing all over again, and the situation was too pathetic to tease him about to any degree. So I just fished nonchalantly, letting hooked fish run to their hearts' content and not rushing to respond to invitations to set the hook. But to no avail. Soon I had 26 fish: my 20 and 6 for Jim.

He did catch some fish, but not near 20. It was a black day for a fine person, especially such a competitive person.

You have seen those movies that have a cast of gods looking down on humans and amusing themselves by making us miserable. I thought of that scene at that time. Poor Jim! Why was Fate unkind to my very best friend? There had to be an explanation. There was.

Luck.

— Who's in Charge? —

The fishery resource at American Lake has not been well-managed over the years, but there have been bright spots. The wielders of power have been and are the state, the military, and the county.

Back a number of years there were times of neglect. The state of Washington had left management of lakes to the 39 counties. So you had county hatcheries, game wardens, and fishing regulations. I do not know the ins and outs of legislative budgeting, but I suspect it was a haphazard matter whether or not the county put how many fish of which species into which lake.

I recall one local legislator who lived in a small town near the Cascades foothills. He became chairman of a committee that had sayso on fish plantings. To what extent he was operating under state or county regulations makes no difference. But he was able to cram a large number of trout into a small lake where he had property, along with some special regulations relating to fly fishing.

I helped him thin down the population of trout one opening day morning by taking either 15 or 20 mid-sized rainbows as I fished in a one-man rubber boat after a night of working in the newspaper mailroom until 4 a.m. There were plenty of fish left over and there were many voters who went away praising the legislator.

What Can We Ruin?

But the main player has been the state, and they have made moves with both positive and negative results. It is easy to criticize because the occasional big errors have been really big and apparent to all.

One time about 20 or so years ago it became apparent to me after getting skunked three times in a row at American Lake, that something was not as it should be. I guess I am especially smart this way. For a few years past I had been taking good catches of lovely 13-and-14 inch kokanee on a regular basis. Then, suddenly, I couldn't buy a fish. Fishing the same way, conditions the same, spitting over my left shoulder into the wind whenever possible, and so forth. I contacted the State Game Department in Olympia, the state capital, and finally found my way via telephone to a college-educated expert on kokanee.

He chatted with me sympathetically and then gave me the explanation I was looking for. We were victims of a "class failure."

Now I don't know what class failure means to you, but I think of some of the kids who didn't pay attention in school and who were graded F and maybe had to repeat that class next year. But that wasn't it, as it turned out.

The expert patiently explained to me that once a year the people from his department put a large number of tiny kokanee in what he described as a barge. I don't know what this conveyance looked like because all other game department plantings I have ever seen have been accomplished by tank trucks that dump many tiny trout into a lake to the delight of bass and seagulls and others.

What the expert apparently meant was that all the little fish that year – each and every one – had given in to disease, predation, lack of oxygen, or some other calamity. I found this almost too weird to believe, so I chose not to believe it. Out of the very large number of fish supposedly planted, you would suspect that maybe one or two survived and could at least give me the courtesy of a nibble, just for old time's sake.

I think it more than likely that there was no plant of fish at all or that someone put them in the wrong lake, or whatever.

The Trust Has Rusted

Ordinarily, I am not a person who dislikes government per se. I pay my taxes, try not to speed on the highway, and generally do a good job of obeying laws and voting for those I deem the best scoundrels on the ballot. But the state pulled a boo-boo many years ago that made many of us wonder. In the meantime, they have changed the names of responsible bodies and have gone through a succession of department leaders so that only a few of us survivors seem to remember. And please don't tell anyone where we live.

At that time – I believe this started in the 50s – the fishing public became enamored of a selective poison called rotenone. Most everybody wanted to fish for salmon and trout. To hell with perch and bass and bluegills and all those sticky-rayed fish, the thinking went.

The beauty of rotenone was that you could kill every fish in a lake if you applied the poison correctly. Game Department people in outboards patterned a lake with chemicals from gunny sacks and the fish choked and floated to the top. Fortunately, the fish were still edible, and many delighted people and seagulls scooped up free meals.

Lakes freed from their fish populations could be planted with lots of tiny trout that would safely grow up without worry from being eaten by ambitious bass and perch. So, many lakes were rotenoned and planted with rainbows and other trout.

I recall being in college when these poison-and-plant operations were rolling. Clear Lake near Eatonville was selected as a worthy site. The lake was poisoned and replanted.

Fish Cakes and Rye Bread?

"Let's go out to Clear Lake and see what is happening," one of my college classmates suggested. So we piled into his car and drove about 30 miles into the lovely green countryside. There were four or five of us and all were gung-ho for the wonderful thing we were going to see. When we got to the lake we jostled one another to get out of the car first and out onto the dock.

There we saw a wonderful thing. One of our group had brought a couple slices of Wonder Bread. He tore off some small chunks and flung them off the end of the dock. Wow! The water boiled as the hungry fish, just a few days from opening day, tore into a meal unlike any they had seen since the nice man at the hatchery had thrown them pellets every day on a precise schedule.

We all got to Clear Lake on opening day along with what seemed to be a majority of the county population. You could not quite walk across the lake, stepping from boat to boat, but it was close to that. And most of the trout dived for the bottom and decided to go hungry for a while longer until things quieted down.

No doubt this mass management of the fish populations pleased the people in general. Little lakes with catfish and stickleback plus two resident trout became a place where Little Jimmy could go with Grandpa and hope to land a real trout with his new spinning reel and rod. Most people didn't know what to do with a spiny rayed fish, anyway. All those stickers and bones, and most of them didn't jump when you got them on your line.

American Lake was huge compared to most other lakes in our area. It presented problems for the rotenone treatment. For one thing, it had a creek coming in as well as those springs out in front of the boathouse. It had a few muddy inlets where an enterprising bullhead catfish might burrow in and hide.

Then there was the resistance of some old-time anglers who appreciated bass and perch. Those stood by and grumbled and some of them sneaked a few of the banished fish back into the water as soon as they got the chance.

An Underwater Garden

The water in American Lake has always been clear and looks clean. From time to time, tests have showed bacteria that alarmed health authorities, but in the main the water is still transparent.

You can see some distance down into the depths on the right kind of sunny day. But what you see now is not what you used to see. There is an underwater growth of weeds, about everywhere you go. These plants reach up from the bottom and get to the surface in a few areas, such as the "sunken island" near the point with the military sign.

Since American Lake has been rotenoned that long time ago, growth of aquatic weeds has spurted. It is likely there are depths in the lake where it is too deep for enough sunlight to penetrate for the weeds to get optimal growth. I don't know. But I do know the weeds do well in water, say 50 feet or so deep.

This weed growth provides cover for small fish and promotes other aquatic life such as insects. So it is not a bad thing. My point is that it is just different from what American Lake used to be like. And I liked the way it was. But I like the way it is, too.

Those who troll for fish, either salmonoids or spiny ray, will try to come close to weed beds without getting tangled. This gives fish of all sizes the opportunity to hide and then dart out to grab that juicy crankbait or mealworm.

So I cannot make a judgment on how the lake poisoning worked out. The fish are bigger on average now. In recent years, while trolling for kokanee, catches of 13 and 14-inch fish are routine. Those used to be trophy size.

Thank You, Officers

The agents who work for the game department, fisheries, the wildlife division or whatever they call those agencies, are not unfriendly. They seldom appear and even less often check to see if an angler has a valid license. But it is nice to chat a little with them from time to time as they pursue their rounds.

In order to see an agent, you might consider going out on opening day on a Sunday and not too early, say after 8 a.m. I have had my license checked about 3 or 4 times in more than 60 years, and it has almost always been after 9 a.m. at American Lake.

Usually, the agents are just fishing for a little more information from anglers and they are also letting everyone know they actually do get out on the water once in a while, so beware if you are doing something not quite legal.

I recall times before I got a fish finder – that electronic marvel that shows where fish are swimming below your boat – and seeing a couple of officers trolling American Lake just as I was. They helpfully volunteered that they had been picking up groups of fish at 30 feet depth, crucial information for someone with brains enough to use it. But this was before I learned that this is the optimum depth for trolling American Lake most of the time and all things being equal.

For a number of years, the owners of Bill's Boat House – the successor of Dittemore's and Don's – raised a number of rainbow trout in pens adjacent to their docks. This appeared to boost the trout fishery, especially the size of some of the lunkers. I have not heard anything about this program for a few years now. It was a cooperative venture with the state fisheries people, and I do not know what happened to what seemed to be a good idea.

The fishery at American Lake has been good for some years now, provided we have no more "class failures" or planting fish in the wrong lake. Since the state has taken over management of the waters, it appears that fishing has generally improved. The catch limits have gotten smaller and more waters are open year around. I hope we are not headed to a catch limit of two or a catch-and-release only fishery.

One of the joys of fishing is knowing that you may catch a fish and be able to take it home to eat. A hopeful fisherman tends to be a happy one.

— A Few Fish Stories —

Since I went fishing in American Lake so many times over so many years, it would have been remarkable if I had not made a memorable catch from time to time. Many years of catching mainly small kokanee and rock bass and perch were routine. Then there were the years of virtually no kokanee at all due to the State Game Department's ignorance or duplicity, I never figured out which.

For a number of years after college, I had the pleasure of knowing Paul Harkonen. Paul was a talented photographer, educated gentleman, and a Finn, all at the same time. He had no patience with men who did not appreciate fishing and hunting. When co-workers at Weyerhaeuser started to tell about their latest round of golf, he had a way of bringing them up short with, "How many did you catch?"

The one time I took Paul fishing at the lake with me in the little tub of a wooden boat I had at that time, we caught very little except the line of another angler crossing in a path perpendicular to ours.

Paul represented the practical side of angling to me: not only how many of what kind did you catch, but what size were they and how did they taste after they were fried.

Is it a Scandinavian thing? The Swedish family that used to rent our largest boat so they could put four or five handlines into the water were obviously more interested in eating than in sport. I don't know, but if it is so, there is a bit of Scandinavian blood in most of us. Oh, you get the "purists" who fish only with the tiniest dry flies and immediately release all they catch with a supercilious smirk and sidelong glance at the rest of us.

This attitude was paramount in the book and movie, "A River Runs Through It," in which a superior preacher's two boys joined Daddy in dry fly fishing and looking down on the rest of us, except they did keep much of their catch for eating. Oh, they were so superior to us worm-drowners that it was a holy thing to behold.

But I digress; wouldn't you know. We were going to brag a bit about catching poor defenseless fish.

Not Very Big at All

Even though I fished American Lake many times more than other bodies of water, I netted a much smaller percentage of larger fish from my favorite lake. Nothing I ever hooked in American Lake came near in size to two beauties I took from nearby Gravelly Lake one evening while fishing with my old journalism teacher and friend Homer Post. Those lovely rainbows measured 21 1/2 inches and 24 1/2 inches and weighed 3 pounds, 12 ounces and 5 pounds, 12 ounces. I am not ashamed to say they were caught with the aid of a two-spoon troll and big, juicy angleworms.

But I never caught a fish near that big from American. I may have hooked into one on a summer's morning in front of the boathouse. I am not sure of how large that fish was, but it was a dandy big rainbow, or possibly a cutthroat. It seized my bait while I was fishing in the usual spot over the springs in front of the boathouse. The fish came straight up and rolled on the surface.

Bob Firch was nearby. He and others watched while the large fish spat out my bait and went on to a luncheon date elsewhere. I was stunned to the point that I did not really realize the magnitude of what had happened. "That fish must have been 15 or 16 inches long," I managed to mutter in Bob's direction when my heart had slowed down a bit and I had automatically pulled in my line to replenish the bait.

"It was a lot bigger than that," said Bob, probably thinking that God had sent that fish to the wrong hook instead of one where an experienced angler with developed skills would have had a better chance of landing it.

A Catch to Remember

It was many years later while I was fishing with Bill Collings, a friend from work, when I finally took an 18-inch cutthroat as Bill and I enjoyed a sunny mid-morning while stillfishing near the point off the Soldiers' Beach.

We anchored in a good spot. I had located a number of good spots around the lake, some gooder than others. This particular one was located by rowing just so far south and east of the point at one end of the large cove some called The Culvert. A big log from an old fir tree stretched horizontally along the beach. A certain distance out from that log was a good place.

After we anchored and found bottom, we started in on cookies and warm coffee after tossing over a couple of spoonfuls of feed eggs. The eggs seemed to be sending up their oil slicks sooner than if they had settled to the bottom 30 feet or more down. This indicated that something was happening much closer to the surface than usual. Since we were not getting any bites, I decided to experiment a bit and I took off my splitshot sinker and buried a salmon egg as completely as I could in the small hook. This I tossed over the side and watched as it descended at a rate similar to the spoonful of feed eggs that followed.

This is not an unusual situation. Big trout sometimes locate a boat whose occupant is throwing out samples of cuisine. So the large fish swim around in the area just under the boat and help themselves to the goodies destined for the bottom.

Soon my line was paying out and my pole was jumping as a cutthroat of a larger than usual size felt the hook and started a trapeze act. He jumped and sent spray flying as I grabbed the line with my left finger tips and lifted the pole skyward with my right hand, being careful to secure the line between the cork grip of the rod and my right fingers and thumb.

Uncle Oscar had taught my brother Paul and me to strip line from the get-go. "You touch that reel and I'll break your arm," he warned as we played our first catches. He indicated that the reel was pretty much for winding up the line for storage after we were through fishing for the day and then unwinding it when we went out again.

Stripping the line gives the maximum in feel to the angler. It also provides the greatest control when the fish suddenly rockets away with chunks of line or when it is bending the rod as the lucky angler works it in toward the net.

So I alternately stripped the line in and let it slip out between my fingers and the cork grip until the large cutthroat gasped exhausted on its side. When Bill slipped the net under the fish, I felt relief at not losing it and gratification at catching it. It measured 18 or 19 inches long and was indeed a cutthroat instead of a rainbow.

You Win, You Lose

Just around the point that runs out into the lake to the northeast of where this catch was made, I had an experience with another larger trout, presumably also a cutthroat.

You remember, I suppose, my telling you about the box of old tackle in the shack that I had raided. Among my yield there was a star drag reel, and I was using it to fish near shore not long after I started my job at the lake.

I made a short cast – the only kind I was capable of – and started to pull on the oars so that the flatfish on my leader would swing around to follow as I trolled along the shoreline.

Wham! A good trout smacked the plug and leaped into the air. But, unlike my reaction when stripping line, I could not react fast enough or effectively enough. How in hell do you work this complicated piece of machinery?

Now, any of you oldtimers who have a star drag reel understand just what I should have done, but I had no idea of what that was.

So I could not let line out to coincide with the fish's runs, and as a consequence, I lost the trout.

Changing Targets

But this is supposed to be about catching fish, not losing them. Most of the larger fish we saw when anglers came in to the boathouse after their outings were smallmouth bass. It took me a while to zero in on that marvelous species, and I have to give Jim credit for developing my interest.

We caught lots of spawning perch and chunky little rockbass from our hole in the dock. One time I caught a silver by letting a salmon egg lie on the bottom and then hoisting a startled 11-inch kokanee out onto the dock before it had time to put up a fight.

But we knew there were lots of other fish in the lake. So few men were able to go fishing because of their employment in war industries that, as Jim put it, "I bet every dock has at least one nice bass under it." He had learned about bass by fishing at his sister's place on Spanaway Lake, so I learned from him.

We started out by rowing slowly along the shoreline. Behind us we dragged a worm or part of a worm with very little or no weight on the leader. We got numerous strikes and caught some rockbass this way, plus a few small bass. Once in a while we would stop at a dock or float and fish around the edges with our angle worms.

In that wartime there was little or no manufacturing of fishing tackle because everything was given over to the war effort. So the leader we could buy was old and brittle. You could snap a 4-pound test with your young hands, and the leaders broke when we hooked small and medium-sized bass and tried to hoist them onto a dock. In fact, we never caught anything as much as a foot long.

But we did admire the bass. They were so pugnacious. A little bass four inches long would dart out from under a dock and attack a plug larger than itself. The ones eight and ten inches long would grab and run with an angleworm piece. They would throw themselves with abandon into the air, and they seemed to be magical at coughing out a worm and hook after being hooked fairly well.

A Lunchtime Show

It was a long time before I caught a decent-sized bass from my favorite lake. But I had developed a fun way to fish for these powerhouses.

In the water, a smallmouth looks olive drab with darker stripes on its body. Most anglers cannot distinguish it from a largemouth, but it is generally smaller and more slender.

In spring I rapidly found that the bass hung along the shoreline in shallow water. Whether they were looking for a place to spawn or were protecting the place where they already had, I did not know. But I rowed the shoreline, trailing a flatfish behind the boat. And I carried a second rod, rigged up and ready to use.

The second rod was my flyrod. I had it within easy reach as I trolled slowly and searched the shallows visually. If I got a strike from a rockbass or perch, then I played the fish on the trolling line, but if I saw a sizable fish, I ducked down as best I could, picked up the flyrod and tossed out a big angle worm or night crawler.

Then I'd hope the fish did not see me or did not care, and there would almost invariably be a strike.

The smallmouth likes to pick up the bait and run a distance with it before turning it around preparatory to swallowing it. So the angler lets the line run out until he guesses it is the right time to strike. Bass have hard mouths, so one hopes the hook penetrates or is swallowed. Then the fight is on.

Just after noon one sunny day, I found myself in the shallow water on the west shore of the Vets' Hospital. I had located a good bass and was lucky enough to get it well hooked. As my boat drifted in toward shore, I realized I had an audience. It was noontime and a number of the employees at the hospital had brought their lunches down to the shore to eat in the sunshine and catch a few rays while enjoying the view.

As usual, the bass put up a good scrap, jumping several times and trying all the bass tricks it could come up with. But I was able to net the tired fish after a few minutes, and I felt triumphant. It measured something like 18 or 19 inches and was the largest bass I had taken at that time.

A Fishing Exhibition

Sometime earlier in my angling career, Jim and I were fishing near the northeast shore of Silcox Island when a large fish broke the surface not far from our boat.

"Don't get too close, fellows," a calm voice entreated us. Then we realized that the fish was on a line coming from a boat anchored just a few feet out from the island shore. A man and a woman were in the boat and they had a bulging gunny sack tied to the side of their boat. The man continued to play the fish while we watched fascinated. The big bass gleamed bronze in the sunlight when it jumped.

The man told us that they had caught four fish that day, totaling 16 pounds. We believed him, and I marked the spot well for future reference.

So I knew the lake held large bass, and I knew where others had caught them. But being the kids we were, we were not "skookum" enough to imitate the successful anglers. We were off to other adventures.

I should mention that the man and his wife took the large bass with livebait, which was then lawful in the state. In fact, Grandpa sold little bait fish for 35 cents a dozen. Most of our minnows were little sculpins, but some were rock bass. I sometimes increased our stock of bait fish by pushing out boats from the shore while holding a short rope from the bow and using a short-handled net to dip up the minnows that had been hiding under the boats.

The little silver trout we caught in the days when the catch limit was 20 fish measuring six inches or longer, were from six to eleven inches in length. This made the catch of a larger fish much more of an occasion.

In later years – much later – the kokanee we caught in the lake were much larger. I took some 5-fish limits of 13 and 14-inch fish but never connected with a really big one, although other anglers said they did from time to time.

When we were kids, the limit was 20 fish, then 15 later on, then 12, and ultimately 5. I suppose someday it will be 2 or 1 or maybe catch and release. The flyfishermen who consider themselves so superior might like that. They could catch and release large numbers of fish, many of which would die. Then they could go to the Barbecue Inn in Tillicum and order fish (cod) and chips.

Old Man and the Bass

In my first or second year at the lake, there was one memorable evening with a painful incident.

Usually the boats were all in by dark, which can come pretty late in the summertime. But this one time, there was a boat overdue, and Gramps was concerned. He stood on the shore near the big dock and puffed his cigar as he looked to the south.

Eventually the rowboat came in. A middle-aged man was rowing and an old fellow sat on the back seat and held a handkerchief on his bloody hand. Seems the two of them had been fishing near the small islands when the old guy had somehow managed to impale his hand on a good-sized hook. I have always been squeamish enough, so I did not try to listen to details, nor did I care to look at the old guy's anguish.

But I remember the talk around the boathouse afterward. The old man had been upset – not so much from the pain of the hook in his hand, but he had lost a sizable bass near the largest of the small islands. If you are a fisherman, you will understand.

— Pests of the First Water —

Eden had its snake. And fishing in American Lake had its – perhaps I should amend this so that you won't think I am trying to condemn every waterskier. There are pests and miscreants of all kinds frequenting the waters of American and other lakes.

There was a time when I would have gladly signed a petition to establish an open season on waterskiers. Such a sporting event would have to be fair: shotguns only with size 6 shot and no fair aiming at anyone 75 yards or more away. There would have to be a license and a report of successful shots with trophies awarded yearly.

Now I have come to realize in my dotage that not all waterskiers are undesirables. It seems there are fewer each year and they are now getting a dose of their own medicine from a much worse lot: so-called personal watercraft.

Me First and Only

The best description of most pests on the water is that they are thoughtless or perhaps brainless. Dad throws them the keys to the speedboat and goes back to the stock market page. Of course his children have been taught manners and consideration of others. Or have they? To an observer, it may appear that no one on waterskis gives a damn about anyone else's enjoyment. Besides, Dad himself is often the worst offender as he indulges his lust for speed regardless of anyone else.

Little enough regard is given to the wakes trailing behind the powerful motors required for water skiing. Smaller boats and canoes are often endangered by these walls of water. Sometimes those running these speedy machines are often too young or not qualified in any other respect.

This is, of course, not fair to some people who just go along with the rest of the crowd or perhaps even give some thought to others. I have even met polite and considerate personal craft operators. This has pleased and astonished me.

The main effect people who tool up and down the lake in a scary if not outright dangerous manner has had on me is to hasten my style of fishing toward trolling rather than stillfishing. When you are trolling, you may move out of harm's way, but when anchored and stillfishing, you are vulnerable in the extreme.

Oh, how the old boys out in front of the boathouse used to cuss anyone who caused even a mild wake that disturbed their fishing. But that was a day when gas was short and perhaps brains were more prevalent, although some of these same guys thought the artillery practice at nearby Fort Lewis was causing poor fishing as well.

When Jim and I had our two glorious years at American Lake, there were maybe three or four luxury speedboats total on the lake. One enterprising fellow had an electric motor – he must have made it himself – run off a car battery. I heard him one time as he complained about a speedboat that nearly cut his line. "There are times," he said, "when I have two hundred or so feet of line out."

Good luck to him today. But one might say he was the one being inconsiderate. What was he fishing for? Tarpon or swordfish? But it is easy enough even for a nitwit to see that a slowly trolling boat has a line out behind it and that this should be no incentive to try to run over that line.

Accidents, My Foot

There have been "accidents" on American Lake. A little girl lost a leg to an outboard motor near the National Guard beach. A boater crushed a kayak with a young man in it, giving him terrible injuries. On and on. Careless people who don't give a damn operate in a careless manner and the law, at best, slaps them lightly on the wrist or bottom. Anglers hurrying to a better fishing spot are not always considerate of others either.

A number of people have drowned in the lake because of their own or someone else's negligence. Some parents allow kids too young to drive to tool up and down the lake with no supervision, only tacit approval. Obviously, policing of the waters is needed. But aside from the "crash boat" that the Army kept on the lake during the war, you won't see any speed cops. Pity.

I do not miss the personal watercraft and their skilled drivers doing curly-cues near where I am trying to fish. Not having to cope with them is one of the joys of old age and not being able to fish anymore.

In years past, I have been narrowly missed while in a small aluminum pram with a 90-year-old fishing companion as a waterskier whipped close to the island shore in pursuit of a thrill. Most often, however, it is just a matter of riding the waves and thinking evil thoughts as some inane youngster thinks you are enjoying the athletic and beautiful spectacle he/she provides.

I do wish for safer waters for future recreational users. The scullers and rowers are the best, and they deserve consideration from others. The seaplanes are no problem at all. Pilots have to exercise caution as part of their trade.

Sorry to sound like a preacher, although Grandpa liked to hear them over the radio.

— Fishing Partners —

There are two ways I enjoyed fishing: alone or with someone else.

Do not make me chose between these alternatives; they are both the whipped cream atop the strawberry shortcake of life.

Again, I would not want to pick my favorite among all the fine individuals who have joined me in fishing ventures. But, of course, there are some who stand out. Let me tell you some of the things that came to pass while fishing with others.

Of course, my lifelong friend James A. Hutson is the first to consider. Jim was my alter ego in our high school days. We were about the same height and both had dark hair. We were far from identical, but people mixed us up anyway from time to time.

Jim and I first became friends in junior high school when we played a mild form of hooky and slipped off early one spring day to go fishing in Chambers Creek. He pedaled his bike and I rode on the handlebar. It seemed we had similar roles as we got older. He was always there to help me.

What's Up, Dock?

About the best thing I ever did for Jim on a short list was that he became my frequent guest as we fished in American Lake. We dropped off to sleep on cots in the little shack with the Pepsi sign on top and the Coke advertisement on the wall inside.

As we settled down for the night after a day of fishing and frittering away our time on or near the dock, we closed our eyes and chatted. "What are you seeing?" Jim asked. "Perch," I replied, "lots and lots of perch swimming around our bait."

This was to be expected since we had spent hours kneeling down to shield our eyes and peer at our worm-covered hooks being inspected by the schools of yellow perch under the dock. We caught a lot of those perch and they paid us back by emblazoning images on our minds. They supplanted girls and baseball games and everything else as we drifted off for the night.

Jim remained a lifelong friend. There were years when we did not see each other for a long time. But when we met up again, it was always as if we had never been apart.

We played at sports together. Jim was heavier and a tad bigger than I. When we turned out for football in high school, he aimed to be an end. He was fast enough and gave it a good try, but there was too much competition. I found the same thing as I turned out for quarterback. My lack of size did not help, and I could not convert my success in sandlot touch football to the varsity level, We gave up football at length, except for touch intramural games when we were at College of Puget Sound together. We played, and not too badly, for the Independents, my "political party" in later years.

We both served as best men at our first weddings. We both had brief careers as school teachers after college, even though we shook our heads at some of the inane courses and bumbling instructors we encountered.

Jim first taught at Randle, a rugged little town in the Cascade foothills south and east of Tacoma. He fished the Cispus and Tilton and little trout streams in the area and learned to hunt – something he introduced me to when we were still young.

A Real Partner

There is not enough ink to tell you all about Jim. He did leave teaching early on and wound up as a successful insurance salesman. As a measure of his success, he owned his own building in Tillicum and occupied only part of it in his business, renting out the remainder.

But we were talking about fishing, weren't we? And Jim and I must have fished together at least a hundred times, counting dock fishing, trips at American in Gawley's boats, hiking and camping out in the mountains, salmon fishing at Neah Bay, and wetting our lines at Mineral, Bay, Horseshoe, Silver, and many other lakes.

Jim was a perfect fishing partner. It was never hard to consider how or where we would fish. One of us would suggest a venue or a method, and agreement was never far behind.

The thing that made Jim a great partner was that he was competitive, in his own mild way, but he was also unselfish. We were always glad to see the other catch fish, large and small.

Jim did have a form of palsy – I think that is what it was – that made his hands tremble constantly. This presented problems in tying leaders to lines. He patiently suffered through this handicap and never complained.

During one of our teen years there occurred a period of separation from Jim. He had the opportunity to spend some time in Alaska, I believe with a relative.

He wrote and made the numeral 17 especially large and underlined it when he told of catching a long Dolly Varden. I had not even seen a Dolly Varden at that time, so he was one up on me.

A Big Bomb, Boys

Jim and I were together fishing in the mountains when the atom bomb was dropped on Nagasaki and Hiroshima. We were informed of the good news by Jim's dad Doc when he came to pick us up in his borrowed Model A on the mountain road at Summit Creek, just a few miles from Ohanapecosh Hot Springs. The Hutsons had invited me to make the trip to that landmark with them. The old folks stayed at the lodge and enjoyed the mineral waters while Jim and I hiked, camped, and fished up Summit Creek to Jug and Fryingpan lakes and a little further.

"We dropped a really big bomb on the Japanese," Mr. Hutson said. The news barely sunk in on us, fatigued, sunburned, and mosquito-bitten as we were after three nights camping at Jug Lake and environs. But a few days later back home, Jim hauled out his trombone and we were joined by Dick Tibbitts and a few others from Jim's neighborhood on V-J Day as we contributed to the general euphoria by standing on Yakima Avenue and hollering and making a little noise.

Jim and I spent our college days together at then College of Puget Sound in Tacoma. I don't remember being in a class with Jim, but we spent a lot of time together on campus and off. He had managed to stay out of the service but was working his way through school. I was fortunate to have the G-I bill from my brief Army service.

Besides intramural football and basketball at school, we continued to fish here and there. One time we collected Douglas fir cones to sell to Weyerhaeuser from their land near Snoqualmie. We fished in the river – I think it was the Tolt – and he caught a 14-inch Dolly and I took a 14-inch rainbow. Slight edge to me since a rainbow is generally considered to be a better fish than a Dolly.

I mentioned Jim introducing me to hunting. He was standing side by side with me the first time I shot a deer. He fired first and missed. I was lucky that my shotgun slug hit a dandy forked-horn blacktail deer in a perfect spot. It was a long shot and was the only time I ever shot a slug from a shotgun. I felt as if I had been hypnotized or as in a slow-motion dream. Jim was laughing so hard as he skinned the deer that he cut through the hide a few times and made holes here and there. His perpetually shaking hands didn't help either, but at least he didn't injure himself.

An Athlete to the Last

My athletic career did not go very far. Early marriage squelched any idea of playing college baseball. Intramural was it. And Jim and I played slowpitch some years later.

But he could not give up the idea of competing and he played and coached several sports up to the time of his untimely death after a heart bypass and a knee replacement that finished him.

I visited Jim three out of the last four days of his life, including the day before he died. His death shocked us all, but his battling to the end was no surprise.

The Romantic View

Jack Wilkins was a writer and a longtime friend. We worked at the local newspaper and both worked for Weyerhaeuser. We camped on the Grand Ronde River in southeast Washington once for a memorable few days with another newspaper buddy.

Jack was a stringer for The New York Times and he was a really good writer. He had worked for the Lewiston, Idaho, paper and had spent some time as a sheepherder in the mountains of Idaho.

Jack and I fished together seldom, but enjoyably. I remember, in particular, one trip to American Lake.

I had been knocking the silvers dead stillfishing. After years of perfecting this activity, I had it down to a science. So I enjoyed taking numerous people out to the lake and showing them how it was done. A limit of 15 kokanee and rainbows mixed was not an unusual occurrence to me. But, it turned out, Jack was not impressed.

First of all, Jack was a steelhead fisherman and a good one. When we camped on the Grand Ronde, he nailed a couple of beauties of eight or ten pounds each. I never could catch those damn things and never even had one on my line.

Secondly, and most importantly, Jack was a romantic. I should have known this by his writing. Also, he tried rather successfully to look like Ernest Hemingway, full beard and all. He smoked a pipe and looked thoughtful without trying.

I carefully explained our modus operandi as I lowered the anchors after being sure we were in the exact spot I wanted to be. We were in between the second-largest island in the lake and the point with the military sign. Just about half way, that is, and where the water was exactly as deep as I wanted it to be.

We had our flyrods rigged up with level flyline and three-foot leaders of three-pound test with number nine Octopus hooks baited with caddis fly larva. I found bottom for one rod and then the second one, just to save time and not risk Jack's being too leisurely or being unable to do the act just right.

Then I tossed over the feed eggs on the side of the boat we were fishing. We both fished on the same side and with the sun to our backs.

"Pull up anywhere from two to twelve inches," I instructed in my best Guide from the Big Woods voice. I said, "Now rest your rod on the gunwale and hold onto the line with your left hand while keeping your right hand ready on the grip so you can set the hook when you see a bite."

I thought I heard a sigh. Did I? Then quiet as the early morning sun climbed just a little and the swallows zipped over our heads. Was that sigh the first sign of a rebellion? I hoped not.

Pretty soon things got tense. Wiggles. Jack was stretching or fiddling with his pipe. The boat rocked a little and the rods moved up and down just a bit with the rocking.

"You have to sit still," I muttered. "These things bite really light most of the time, and you can't tell if you are getting a bite if the boat is going up and down."

Silence. Then a slight dip in my rod and I was on it like a tiger. I swiftly lifted the rod with my right hand, while holding the line coming off the reel with the fingers of my left hand. The bamboo rod arced as I set the hook and stripped in line quickly to keep a tight hold on the fish.

The silvery beauty sped to the surface and leaped in a shower of droplets. I held the line tight and followed the fish's plunge back into the water, where it headed away from the boat as fast as it could. I have often wondered what a fish thought when that delicious morsel of food suddenly became a force restricting movement. Fish are not usually as smart as the average angler, I think, but they sometimes act as if they have some intellect.

My fish this time made a couple of runs. I had to pay out line between my thumb and fingertip as the fish pulled some of my line back through the guides. The trick was to keep a constant pressure on the line as it ran between thumb and forefinger. A decent fish can keep you occupied playing line in and then out in a controlled manner until the battle is over. The fish lies gasping on its side and the long-handled landing net is slipped under another prize.

Beauties of Nature

A fresh-caught rainbow trout or kokanee taken from a pristine lake has to be one of the most beautiful sights of nature. The kokanee is such a bright silver that it outgleams a new dime or your mother's Sunday-dinner silverware. A rainbow is dark above, light below and has a red line running its length from tail to head on its sides. The fish are colored beautifully and differently depending on the lake they came from. Perhaps there is some interbreeding with cutthroat trout that will make your rainbow more speckled than usual. The combination of factors, genetic and environmental, that affect how a particular fish may look are complex. But they are all gorgeous.

So, after taking three or four kokanee while Jack watched, it was time to move on. We didn't need more fish to eat at the time. Besides, the bites were beginning to be more scarce. There is no getting away from the fact that early mornings are the best time to fish, at least most of the time.

So Jack spoke. I was interested in his reaction. This experienced fisherman had landed any number of fresh steelhead. He grew up in New York state and I heard the fishing was good there. He fished the streams and big lakes of Idaho before moving to Tacoma. His opinion was valued.

"I am wondering: Could we do something that is a little less computerized?," the big fellow intoned.

I knew what he meant. He wanted to drift near shore where he could cast a fly or spoon or plug up under the overhanging branches, just to see if there were a lunker trout waiting for a bug to fall out of the heavens. If so, perhaps there would be a brief, heroic struggle. Perhaps the fish would win and the fisherman would say to himself and to the world, "Migod did you see that monster? He must have weighed eight or ten pounds. Wow! What a thrill!"

Jack was killed in a mountaineering accident when he was still a big, powerful man. He watched me tying a few sloppy flies one day not long before his demise and remarked that I could still see so well. It was obvious that he was sad about getting older. Even the strongest have to give it up sometime. I believe he would have chosen to go quickly, as he did, rather than settle down to a computerized way of life.

Tweed Suits Me

I met Norm Tweed through a fellow I thought I knew and one who knew him well. Does that make sense?

Norm taught biology at a nearby community college. I was palmed off on him by another instructor at the college who I had thought went to college with me and my brother Jack. Not so. When I called the teacher and tried to line him up to go fishing, he referred me to Norm. Norm was, and is, a red-hot fisherman.

Subsequently, Norm and I fished a lot together. We camped out in the mountains near Mt. St. Helens before it blew its top. We went salmon fishing at Neah Bay with Jim Hutson and another friend. We fished the Cispus River and a little lake near Onalaska where I lugged my aluminum boat a quarter mile up a trail to catch eight-inch brookies. We hiked in to Manastash Lake with Bob Vance and took a number of the sizable and lovely brookies there.

Wherever I fished with Norm, he was great. He was as unselfish as one could be. He would give you the best fishing hole and share a generous portion of the big trout he had smoked. We traded off trips in my Travelall and his van. We bought each other meals at rural stops along the way to our camping destinations.

One More Trip

So I was sorry to fish at American Lake only one time with Norm. I had not seen him for some time when I ran into him at Patterson Lake near Olympia and invited him out a few days later.

At the time, near the end of my days of fishing at American Lake, I had been doing well trolling for 13-and-14 inch kokanee. The limit was only five by then, and it was not unusual to take that number of fish in a short time.

I had my usual rig ready to go. It was just right for the kind of fishing I was doing. The rod was sturdier than you might like, but I got a good fight out of my fish on it, and it handled a leaded line with an additional ounce and half keel sinker.

The reel was one I had saved up for a while before spending $75 for it. I have never believed reels are the most essential part of tackle, and I strip line whenever possible, but this baby was perfect for the job. I had the drag set just right so that the silvers could take out a little line if needed.

I had broken another rod and in my thrifty way had patched it up. It was not quite as long as one would like and was suitable only for trolling, but it was as good as the reel attached to it. That piece of tackle was an older star-drag that had something busted inside, so you never knew when it would jam up at critical times. I kept this outfit as a backup when I took a guest out to my favorite lake. The guest got to fish with my outfit and I used the broken stuff. Fair enough.

But wouldn't you know, I caught the only two or three fish the day we went out. Norm got skunked and never had a fish on.

Shortly after that trip, I had to give up my boat and trailer. I had become weak with old folks' ailments and it was too difficult for me to go out anymore.

But I remembered the good times with Norm. He was much younger than I and the kind of person who has lots of friends and fishing partners, I am sure.

Captain Courageous

Another of my favorite fishing partners was Bill Collings, who succeeded me as editor of Weyerhaeuser Magazine.

Bill was injured in World War II. He had been a skier in his salad days and enlisted in the mountain troops division. As a result of his injury, he had one of his fingers made into a thumb on his left hand. I don't really remember how many fingers Bill had on that hand, because he got along fine. He typed okay and played piano well and was glad for the invention of the spinning reel, because handling line that way was not too tough.

Bill and I were stillfishing one morning near the Soldiers' Beach when I caught a good cutthroat. It was 18 or 19 inches long. Like all good partners, Bill enjoyed seeing the other guy do well. But we didn't really care much about the number and size of the fish we caught. We enjoyed talking to each other.

Bill had succeeded me in the Weyerhaeuser editor's job, and he wrestled with problems: principally the knotheads he hired to help him. I had no patience with these guys. One of them I had refused to take on as staff writer earlier and, when Bill told me of the troubles this guy caused him, I was sympathetic only to a point.

But we knew the same people, had the same bosses, believed in some of the same things, and got along famously.

Westport, Ho!

I liked salmon fishing all right, but it never compared with trout fishing for me. Nevertheless, I fished in the ocean a couple of times out of Westport. One memorable trip was with Bill and his wife Thelmagene. We stayed at a favorite motel of Bill's and went out in a small charter boat with a skipper named Marion Something.

Bill's idea of a perfect fishing trip included Bourbon and steaks. He and Thelmagene and my wife and I had adjoining motel rooms with a big fireplace between them, and we enjoyed good conversation and sipping.

In the morning, we went out with Marion on his boat. The only other passenger was the wife of a minor celebrity, singer Rusty Draper. She had brought no food with her and was quite upset that she did not catch a fish. Bill, Thelmagene, and Marie did not catch a fish either. I caught a seabass early on. We felt that would be just a start, but it was all we caught.

Bill and I also camped near Morton on the Tilton River. Again, steaks and Bourbon in our tent. For the first time, I noted that Bill was running out of steam. In the early morning when I was anxious to break brush down to the rocky river bank and try for rainbows, Bill opted to stay in the car and get another short snooze. Now, years later, I understand. I could maybe get down to the fishing hole but not back. But at least I can say I have been there.

Bill was a little older than I. He got some form of cancer and he did not have a long, drawn-out sickness, for which I am thankful.

Champion Outdoorsman

As I tell you about some of my fishing companions, I cannot but feel that some of them are worthy of a whole book. There is no way to describe the persona and accomplishments of Robert R. Vance, DDS, in a few words. No one should have as much intellect and talent. It is just not fair to the rest of us.

However, as Fate would have it, Bob and I shared many a fishing trip together. Hunting also, although fishing was always my primary interest. Perhaps this is because it is easier to outsmart a fish than a bear or a deer.

It was my fortune when, in my early 30s, I went to the nearest dentist and it turned out to be Bob. One of my incisors has a minute crack in it and I remarked that this was probably caused by my biting down on a lead splitshot while fishing. We were off and running. What I did not know was that this wiry man skillfully working on my teeth was about as outstanding as one can get in the fields of hunting, fishing, dentistry, and slinging the bull.

There is not enough paper and ink to chronicle all the water and hot air we covered together, but I can say I learned an awful lot from Bob and saw numerous fishing holes I would never have known without his guidance.

In latter years, he hosted me at three and five-day stays in his trailer parked at Sprague Lake in Eastern Washington. There we caught many walleye, a species formerly alien to me, and I lucked onto a 20-inch rainbow and numerous other piscatorial prizes.

There was a time, maybe in the 60s or 70s, when we did not fish often at American Lake because we were up in the mountains or somewhere in Eastern Washington. But then came a time when the rainbows were not difficult to find and they were large enough to merit our attention. They were sprinkled in with a mixture of kokanee and cutthroat – just enough to make it interesting. During those years, we fished fairly often and usually trolled spoons and worms or lures.

Turn Your Back, and . . .

Bob was an enthusiastic trophy hunter. As the years went by, he busied himself chasing varieties of bears and deer up and down mountains in Montana, Idaho, and other states, His travels even took him to areas where he could and did shoot grizzlies and a polar bear. His trophy room was a marvel to behold, chocked full of animals and birds preserved by expert taxidermy.

Meanwhile, I finally learned how to catch kokanee consistently by trolling in my favorite lake. It was late in my fishing career that I dragged Bob out to American on a misty October morning to demonstrate the quality of the kokanee I had been taking.

As luck would have it, it was a little late in the season to expect consistently good fishing. I caught a couple of strong and bright 13- and 14-inchers and Bob got skunked. Fish are no judge of who is on the other end of the line. But he was there to see, primarily, and he had to admit the fish were of good quality.

Bob had a big sense of humor, which added to his charm as a fishing buddy. On one occasion he was driving us around in the mountains near Cle Elum, looking for fish in ponds and streams. We stopped at one particularly beautiful stretch of stream – I think it was the Yakima River.

"Well," he said. "We can't fish here." "Why not?" "I am afraid you might catch a fish," he said and jumped back into his Jeep to tool off on the next segment of our journey.

Another time when we had been hiking in the mountains for some grueling hours and were dog-tired, I stumbled in the twilight on a root in the trail I could barely see. As I flew through the air toward a landing cushioned by a layer of pine needles, my muscles responded. I had muscle spasms in both calves and one shoulder at the same time. This was particularly uncomfortable because you can't rub a leg when your shoulder muscles are screaming for attention.

Bob, who had not yet given up smoking cigarettes, lit one up and leaned on the nearest tree as he inhaled. I don't think he laughed, but he must have been amused near death. He eventually inquired if I had hurt myself, and I cannot repeat my answer.

Generosity Personified

Bob held back on no expense while fishing. When we stayed at Sprague Lake, he always had at least four or five suitable rods and reels with the right kind of line all rigged up and ready to go. My tackle was as good as his. He provided the plugs and bait. We stayed in his house trailer at the resort where he had it parked.

We fished from Bob's trailered boat. He was the best host possible. The only thing I could do in return was buy most of our food. We ate at Shari's or any little restaurant we could find. A couple of times I had to go outside crummy little places to vomit because of the tobacco smoke choking the air inside. I think this amused Bob, who accused me – probably rightly – of a prejudice against the village idiots we sometimes found in these "small rural dives," as Billy Strayhorn might have put it. These rural folk were not uniform. I am sure many of them were bright and perhaps creative, but all seemed to smoke several cigarettes each at one time – is this possible? And I felt as if the cook and owner had hired a middle school kid to stand outside his eight-capacity diner with a sign that said, "Come on in and have a smoke, anyway. You don't have to order anything."

The Rest Thrown In

There were many others who merit mention as fine fishing partners, but they will have to be passed over lightly. Included were three spouses, and all of them had their merits. They all got up at ungodly hours and survived rigors of rough travel. They all were accustomed to bait being stored in the refrigerator. And they all caught fish and acquitted themselves well.

I have taken children fishing, and they all caught fish. These include my own two. Four kids from one family took turns at catching nice rainbows on trolled flies. Their dad was not a fisherman, just a great guy. The three boys and a little girl had a good time and were happy anglers.

Another little guy about eight or ten was a champ. His name was Casey or K.C., or something like that. We went to a lake full of spiny rays and he caught some bluegills. I took a little bass about a foot long. His eyes widened and he confided in me that he didn't think he could handle a fish that size. You have to love a little guy like that.

When I was single, I took a few dates out in my little johnboat. I also invited a couple of my neighbors to cash in on the harvest of silvers at American Lake, but got yawns and shaking heads when I mentioned getting up at 4 a.m.

One Disappoinment

My brother Paul William, sometimes called Billy Paul or Billy or Billy Button Shoeshiner, was the star of my first fishing trip in an actual rowboat. Uncle Oscar took us out to Steilacoom Lake, where he had a friend who loaned him a boat tied up to a dock. The little guy caught two fish: a cutthroat and a silver, while Uncle Oscar took a nice silver. I got skunked for the first, but not the last time. But I was hooked on fishing.

Paul was three and a half years younger than I. We had our scraps as siblings, but we also played sandlot baseball at Whitman Field and enjoyed our version of stickball in our backyard together. We devised all-star lineups that I scrawled on planer ends and kept score as we enjoyed bruising Grandma's irises near the plum tree.

Paul succeeded me for a year or two at the boathouse job when I became sixteen and was eligible to get a job in the shipyards. He helped Grandpa and did his tour of duty at the lake. I left my $40 a month and room and board for a job actually paying $1 an hour. I wore an orange hard hat and rode the South Tacoma bus downtown to transfer to a bus that took us to the Todd Shipyards. Toting my lunchbucket, I passed through the gate, moved the brass that represented me on the time board from out to in, and climbed way up to the deck of the escort carrier we were working on. The rest of my gang were young women and one old man.

Billy and Grandpa Seidelman got along well. But Billy was no fisherman, so I do not know how he passed his time at the lake.

One Strike, Yer Out

Paul said he was looking forward to going fishing with me after his retirement as a very successful shoe salesman. But we picked the worst possible time for our first – and last – outing.

It was in early July and it was hot – either 100 or darn close. So we picked the hottest day and went out to the launch in late afternoon. It was a madhouse. All the parking was gone. I had to launch and leave Paul with the boat while I went back up the road and found a spot.

It took a long time to launch and longer to get loaded up and out of the area. Everybody and his brother were there. The large number of boats whipped the lake into waves. Young lieutenants' wives in huge cruisers whipped by, nearly swamping us and waving in a friendly manner as we swore and yelled at them.

No need to go into more detail. Paul sized up the situation and had another drink instead of another outing. He spent the rest of his life smoking, sipping, watching TV, barbecuing and spoiling the hell out of his grandchildren and neighbor kids alike. Everyone liked him.

I remember some of the fishing times Paul and I had had together. The time the old men returning to the boathouse with a fine catch of trout told us about the shoreline with all the cutthroat waiting for our flatfish is still fresh in my mind. It is too bad we could not have had some more trips together, but our fondest wishes sometimes just don't work out.

All in all, I have been quite pleased with my fishing partners. I thank them for all they have added to my happy life.

— A Game Winning Homer —

"Hold it a minute, I'm getting a bite!"

The speaker was a skinny and wrinkled old man with spectacles and an earnest – almost painful – look on his face. He wore a nondescript hat and a stylish fishing jacket his grandkids had bought for him.

He occupied the rear seat of my little aluminum pram – the one I had bought from Montgomery Ward back in the 60s for ninety-six bucks. He reached out with his pole to hold his bait over the spot where he detected, or thought he detected, a nibble from a fish. I relaxed my grip on the mismatched oars with which I had been about to propel the boat to another fishing spot nearby.

"Could be anything: a rainbow, a perch, a rockbass," the old man muttered. "Let's see if he comes back."

How often have I lived that scenario? And how would I love to live it once again?

But Homer Post is history now. Has been for some years, although he scratched out more than 90 years of life, as much of it taken up by fishing as possible.

Homer was my high school journalism teacher and he became my friend. I took him fishing once in a while as he grew older. He did not have a boat, but he had a nifty three-and-a-half horse Johnson motor that we never took because it was too big and heavy for my little pram. Besides, I always liked to row – up to a point, that is.

A Loyal Wolverine

Homer had attended at least his freshman year at the University of Michigan, and he did not mind telling you about it. In fact, a great many of his stories were about his undergraduate days at Michigan and at Whitman College in Walla Walla. A favorite yarn was about one fine morning when freshman Homer was walking across the Ann Arbor campus and famed football coach "Hurry Up" Yost came steaming in the opposite direction, right past Homer. "Good morning, coach," smiled Homer. "Good morning, young man," said the great man as he poured on the coal in the opposite direction.

That was the entire story. Did you like it?

Or, if the planets were in just the right alignment, Homer might recite the details of the construction of the Michigan football stadium, right from bedrock up. He told of layers of gravel, then soil with particular drainage qualities, then more gravel, etc. It was fascinating. Right up to the grass surface itself.

Pyramid That Story!

As a journalism teacher in those days when newspaper writing was taught in high schools and colleges, Homer was tops. He advised staff after staff of eager high school kids who produced student newspapers that won high and highest national competitive honors.

He taught youngsters how to write down the essentials of a story: the who, what, where, when, why, and how. He demanded that they write stories in an inverted pyramid style, that is, with the most important facts first and the others in descending order.

He insisted that the first word of a story should be a real grabber, whenever possible. No fair starting with "the" or "a" or some such colorless word. He gave samples, which we copied into our notebooks. There were exceptions to rules. One favorite exception was that referring to a criminal named Joe Mahoney, who paid the ultimate price for his transgression.

"A noose of hemp swung Joe Mahoney into eternity," read the Homer-recommended exception to the colorful first word rule.

We learned journalistic terms and all the words needed to steer our way around the printshop. Through cooperation with a commercial printer on South Tacoma Way that printed the school paper as well as the South Tacoma Star, he gave us practical experience laying out pages and directing makeup, reading galley and page proofs and writing fillers. He did a complete job and his students loved him.

Students loved going to the Star premises one night a week during the school year to "put the paper to bed."

His Other Love

Not all his students realized that there was another side of the great teacher. He enjoyed fishing even more than writing for the newspaper and teaching others to write.

And, once again, Fate smiled on me. I became a fishing companion to Homer and I got to listen to him express his beliefs and tell of his experiences while we pursued trout and perch.

Homer had been an athlete. He played end for Whitman in the days when that small school took on Oregon and Washington and other universities. He enjoyed telling of one game when an end for Oregon was allegedly playing dirty and Homer and a teammate got revenge in one way or another.

He had been a baseball player in college, too, and he batted well over .300. Once he showed me a picture of one of the Collins boys – I think it was Eddie – with some other players in baggy baseball pants and with smirks on their mugs. "Now you see why my mother didn't want me to play baseball," he said. "Look at that. Just a little wise guy. Cut you up with his spikes as soon as he would look at you. Oh, I could have gone up to the leagues."

The Bull Runs Wild

What a delight to go fishing with Homer! He was good entertainment for hours on end. And, of all the attributes of a fishing partner, the ability to talk and listen are near the top.

Homer never got tired of telling his stories. And they were just as entertaining the third time around as the first. He rattled off the names of students who had gone on from his classes to responsible jobs with newspapers, AP and UPI, industrial magazines, and government services. They made up a distinguished list, to be sure.

One almost got tired of hearing Homer tell about catching a very large rainbow trout – I think it was about seven and a half pounds – out of Alder Lake near Eatonville.

Homer and Norm Mayer, biology teacher and football coach, had gone up to the relatively new lake created by a big power dam on the Nisqually River. They had high hopes of catching some rainbows or other fish, and I suspect Homer had regaled Norm with the usual fishing yarns.

They paused near the dam so Norm could check his bait and make some slight adjustment to his outfit. Homer did not bother to pull up his yard and a half and worm while Norm rested the oars and concentrated on modifying his tackle. It was quite deep where they were and there was no danger of hanging up on a log or the bottom.

Suddenly the line began screaming off Homer's reel and his pole bent sharply. The battle was on and the old warrior was up to it.

After the traditional long fight, Homer guided the monster fish into the big net they had fortunately taken along with them. It was a fish for the ages and had to be the climax of Homer's long angling career.

Political Opinions

Back to the outing and the old man in the back of my boat. We were anchored near the mouth of Murray Creek and just south of the island near the American Lake boat launch. We were fishing for perch or rockbass mainly, but it was not out of the realm that we might catch a trout or kokanee. And that day we took a foot-long bullhead catfish, a comparative rarity from American Lake.

I confess now, many years after the fact, that I was trying to do a naughty thing. I had smuggled a small tape recorder into the boat in my wicker creel with the intent of recording some of Homer's yarns and opinions.

At that time, Richard Nixon was big in the headlines. Homer hated the mere thought of Nixon and I knew it, so I baited the angler as best I could. We had been discussing politics and Homer had poured out his disdain for the tricky one.

"So," says I. "You wouldn't classify Nixon as one of the greatest presidents?" I could barely keep from laughing out loud.

"What?, that sonofabitch," said Homer. I had hooked him for sure with my query. Homer went on and on about what sort of lowbrow Richard Milhaus Nixon was.

But I began to suspect that Homer was on to me. When I tried to get him to repeat some remarks he had made about a particular Southern Mediterranean ethnic group, he declined. The story he had told me earlier indicated that two or three of the fellows had invaded a primitive but private boathouse on Gravelly Lake and had therein relieved themselves of bodily waste matter. It was a disgusting story, but I was not interested in the story itself but rather how the old journalist told it.

He had an explosive way of hurling invective. One half expected teeth to come flying out from a mouth suddenly reminiscent of "The Scream" of artworld fame.

My efforts were pretty much wasted, however, and I guess it serves me right. The aluminum boat had the wrong effect on the recorder, which faithfully picked up all the noise of oars squeaking, feet scraping on the thin aluminum deck, and so forth. The resultant tape would not win any auditory awards. Indeed, it was hard to understand at all. I still have it and will play it for anyone interested if they will come out from behind the furniture and face the music.

There were other outings with Homer in other lakes. He was my companion the night I caught the two huge rainbows out of

Gravelly Lake after he and I had slaughtered the big yellow perch there in a pleasant late afternoon of fishing.

Many times even I got tired of rowing. Homer would want to go to a spot across the lake. I would row there and we would fish. Like as not the fish would not be biting well. Homer would want to go back across the lake to another spot closer to where we started. And so on. Finally I rebelled mildly. "I'll row," Homer intoned. Oh, sure, I was going to let an 88-year-old skinny man do the rowing. Well, just as I started the trip back, Homer would get a bite. That takes us back to the beginning so to speak. Stop moving those oars and let the man have his bite.

Up a Tree for Now

When I was married to my second wife and living in a big old house bordered by lots of laurel hedge and with lots of roses and trees, Homer used to call me frequently. The purpose of the calls was to beg me to take him fishing, preferably at Alder Lake.

I recall one such call among many. It had become necessary for me to trim off the tops of some very large mature birch trees. I gave myself a pep talk and carefully clambered up to the top of a 16-foot extension ladder so I could use a Swedish bow saw on a trunk that was still plenty thick.

My wife appeared below – way down there. She said Homer was on the line and wanted to talk to me. What should she tell him? I was tempted to hurl myself to death below, but the fall was not far enough, so I said tell him I'll call him back in a little while. After I finished lopping the trees and went into the house. I washed up, made myself a double Manhattan and lay down on our thick and comfortable living room rug to call Homer back. Of course, the message was that the fish up at Alder Lake were biting and he sure would like to wet a line. I was reminded of his dandy three and a half horsepower outboard.

After our talk, I dropped off to sleep right there on the plush rug. I was so tired I did not dream of anything, not even yellow perch swimming around my bait.

One time when I was in my 30s or 40s, I had been taking Homer out to American Lake oftener than usual. For some reason we were not out as early as usual, and it was a sunny day. Of course, early and late hours are almost always best for fishing, but we had no choice. So we trolled for an hour with just a bump or two. Then Homer got in to a good silver. When he pulled it in, he displayed the lure he was using. He held up a thin strip cut from a can of Maxwell Brothers Coffee. It was three or four inches long and about three-eights of an inch wide, painted red on one side and a shiny silver on the other.

Homer had made the lure at home the day before. He punched or drilled small holes in either end and forced a small ringeye onto one end. Onto the ringeye he inserted a small treble hook. The hole at the other end was tied to a leader, which was attached to his monofilament line.

The old angler was proud of himself and with good reason. How many hundreds of dollars had we all spent on fancy lures at Payless Drug Store or Washington Hardware? Homer's lure cost maybe ten cents, probably less.

We started to catch kokanee, one after another on the wonder lure. The fish were only ten feet or so deep, so a light sinker or a couple of split shot got us down to where we wanted to be. With this lure rigged behind a light spinning rod or a flyrod we enjoyed good sport.

An Inventor Honored

We agreed to name the new kokanee killer after its inventor, so the Homer Poster was born. I still have two or three of them in my tackle box and I haul them out from time to time when a change of lures is needed.

The Homer Poster is just one more reminder of my dear old friend and the good times we had together.

Homer and Laura had been married forever. They had two daughters, and Laura always referred to Homer as "Daddy." Laura was as sweet as apple pie, which reminds me of the time when we were out in a boat and Homer seemed about to tell me something racy. When two people are in a boat for hours, they tend to bring out the heavy artillery and tell their innermost thoughts.

We had pretty much solved the world's problems earlier that day. Just as I began to fear Homer would repeat the building of the Michigan stadium or one of the other standard stories I had heard a few hundred times, he strayed into what appeared to be a juicy revelation. "I am a great disappointment to Laura," Homer said as he made some minor adjustment to his tackle.

Oh boy, what was he going to tell me? I held my breath and tried to appear non-committal.

"I don't like pie," Homer said. If I didn't know better, I would have thought the old rascal was pulling my leg.

Another time I heard something about Homer that, while not scandalous, was funny as hell as I visualized it. This from a mutual acquaintance, also a former student of Homer.

Seems Homer and Laura had gone to the Quinault Lodge up on the Olympic Peninsula. They stayed at the lodge for a few days, so Homer could get in some good fishing. The Indians control everything in that area, and you have to buy a special license from them to fish in the lake. Well, Homer could hardly wait to tie into those fish the natives had saved for his sport.

So he got into a canoe and beckoned the love of his life to take a seat in the boat. He would paddle. But first, he listened intently to the latest fishing information some kind soul was dishing out. Homer held onto the dock while Laura stepped.

Alas! Homer's attention wandered just enough so that the lovely Laura, gray hair and specs and all, stepped where the canoe should have been. But Homer had modified his hold on the dock in such a way that Laura stepped first into air and then into water. She came up sputtering and, for the several hundredth time in their wedded life, Homer was glad his bride, daughter of the warden at the federal prison at Walla Walla, where Homer had gone to college, was so mild-mannered and forgiving.

Nevertheless, I just about split as I imagined the plunge and then the cork action to the surface of that dignified lady.

It was sad to see Homer when he came to visit us at the newspaper editorial department as he neared the end. He could not see much, nor hear much, and he had to hang onto a desk for support. People hid behind their computers or quickly went out on errands. They knew the old man was hoping for one more trip to a fishing hole with a sympathetic companion.

Homer, Jim Hutson, Bob Vance, and the others – my favorites among my many American Lake fishing partners and guests – had one important attribute in common.

They were all interesting people who liked to talk and to listen. They all had a love for fishing and the great outdoors.

Now that I cannot go fishing anymore, I miss their company. But I cherish the memories. You don't have to entertain me. I can slump down in a comfortable chair with or without a drink and conjure up the pictures and the feelings of events and people six years past or sixty. You need not call me until dinner is ready or something else equally important is afoot.

— Vignettes —

The cannonball guy and the ironmonger were two regulars of a small group of us who fished often one late summer and fall. We congregated early in the day along the shore near the Vets' Hospital, centered on the dock with the red sign.

Most days we knocked them over, especially the cannonball guy.

He apparently had never heard of sports fishing because he hung a large lead ball sinker over the stern attached to a little spoon of a variety beloved to kokanee. When he got a strike, he horsed his catch up into the boat and quickly got his outfit back in the water. When he got his limit, he ran his electric motor back to the landing and often came out again right away. Sometimes he had a companion with him and could take two limits without a break.

The ironmonger – that is my fanciful name for him – did work in a trade requiring construction and maintenance of metal objects. He was personable. He shared some leaders with me. They had two tiny hooks each and a lighter test leader than I like but they were well tied and conceived.

My trailer and boat – a 14-foot Valco – was old and repairs were often needed. The ironmonger noticed some small but critical welding job that needed to be made on my trailer. He promised a couple of times to bring a portable drill and to perform an alternate operation on my trailer tongue. I am sure he intended to do this, but it was one of those intentions that got buried by time and timing.

Late one morning that year the cannonball guy and the ironmonger and I were rapidly filling our quotas of beautiful kokanee. Nearby and not doing any business at all was a fellow bumbling around. At length, he called out to me and I decided to try to help him. My ironmonger friend and I set him on the right track. The cannonball guy was busy horsing in one fish after another.

"Do you have a dodger?," one of us asked. "Yes." We then proceeded to examine his tackle verbally in all the details and told him how to rig up. We even indicated precisely the best area for trolling, in our collective opinion. That area happened to be right where we were fishing at the time.

A few minutes later, the angler joyously called out, "I got one! Thanks to you guys." He caught some more fish and we left him happy as we took our limit catches to the landing.

Whenever I think of that man, it gives me a warm glow. All he needed was a little guidance, which he was glad to follow. He had a day that made all of us a little happier.

❂   ❂   ❂   ❂

I forgot to mention in the section on stillfishing that a cloth flyline can be a great help in this style of fishing when it comes to stripping the line. The cheaper the line the better. We used to be able to buy level no-taper line quite cheaply.

The flyline gives a good grip, even when your hands are wet, and it does not cut flesh as a monofilament may. If you use the latter it is better if the test is higher rather than lower to minimize the cutting of fingers.

❂   ❂   ❂   ❂

If you ever do fish with periwinkles – and I hope you try them – you should know that they will hatch out eventually. Guys who have left their bait in a warm car have been surprised to find a number of big brown bugs flying around inside.

These caddis larva develop slowly when kept cool. They develop wings to warn you they may fly soon. They are still good bait, although they get softer then.

Also about fishing with periwinkles: One reason Jim and I did so well with them is that they resist a casual bite really well. An angle worm will let a fish pull off part of the bait – not a winkle. So the fish often bite repeatedly on one periwinkle in an attempt to eat it or get it off the hook.

I picked up a few winkles from time to time in certain spots of the lake shallows. These spots were close to shadows cast by nearby trees. The larvae sometimes make cases of wood rather than pebbles. And, in streams, they attach themselves to large rocks – sometimes in considerable numbers – before growing their wings and abandoning their shells for flight.

❂   ❂   ❂   ❂

I usually use three-pound test leader for stillfishing and fly-fishing also. For trolling, I like six-pound test. I believe the lightness of leader to prevent detection by the fish is over-rated and it is better to have strong enough leader to give confidence.

Some guys may like to brag about catching a seven-pound trout on a one-pound test leader, but I award no points for that. Motion of the lure as in trolling is a good cover for the angler, as is the riffling of the lake surface by the breeze. A little riffle will hide your leader just fine.

❂   ❂   ❂   ❂

One morning Jim and I started to fish and the silvers responded right away. It was hard to get our bait down to the bottom before the telltale twitch of rodtips demanded our reaction. We pulled in fish after fish in rapid order. Then, suddenly as the sun began to penetrate the depths, the bite slowed. But Jim and I still managed to catch more fish than the other anglers.

We had spotted our landmarks in four directions and agreed just where to drop anchor. This we did, and soon our baited hooks were where we wanted them and we tossed in some feed. I should mention here that chumming material was not always just feed eggs, which were relatively expensive. Anglers used oats, cream corn, and other ingredients to mix with the immature salmon eggs that made up the purchased stuff. This was usually flung overboard from a tablespoon or some such.

The spot over the springs gets crowded. No one knows exactly where the springs are, but the general area is public knowledge. And you can tell who is closest by who is busiest catching fish, putting out the net every few minutes and wasting no time between bites with the ritual of rinsing hands, wiping them with an old towel, and quickly rebaiting and getting one's hooks over the side.

In order to play a fish, which may pull straight down, race quickly to the top, or head in any direction, it is desirable to have some space between boats. There is no law to enforce this, but it is pretty obvious that this is so.

So we were pretty well packed in when a couple of bimbos in one of Gawleys' boats arrived on the scene. They were about as rude as you would desire. They saw we were catching fish so they wanted to get to the hot spot.

As they pulled up to just a few feet from our rod tips, I called out to them. "You're too close to us. You need to move off a few feet." But what did a young punk of junior high age know? Not much. So these guys just barged in and dumped their anchors.

We continued fishing and catching. Some of the other boats were connecting, too. And the intruders caught a fish or two. Then one of them had a problem. His line became taut between his rod and our anchors. The fish on his line had wrapped around one of our anchors – a not unusual happening under the circumstances.

Pull Up or Shut Up

When a fish decides to swim around an anchor line, the thing to do is pull up the anchor in question and try to capture the fish. This is not a happy chore, since the anchors are heavy and the ropes are out at least 40 feet. This occasions some sweating and a few cross words at times.

Or, you can do what the bimbo had to do. Break off your leader by pulling on your line and attach a new leader and bait so you can continue your day's fishing.

Soon a plaintive voice was calling out. "I think I may be stuck on your anchor rope." "Yes," I agreed as I yanked at my rod and missed hooking a fish. A few more words were exchanged and it became evident that I was not going to pull up our anchor to accommodate this rude person.

Others anchored around chuckled and nodded in approval as the ignorant intruder got his comeuppance.

❂   ❂   ❂   ❂

The reason I did not mention Dave Roalsvig in the section of fishing partners was that he never fished American Lake with me. But he was a doozy. Dave worked in the advertising section of the local newspaper when I was employed there too.

He was a bachelor, jovial, and very much alive. He took up fly fishing and purchased a complete outfit of Scientific Anglers brand tackle. I told him about our many recent limit catches in some local lakes by dragging flies. He was eager to see how this was accomplished but he could not help but ridicule my cheap tackle, including a level flyline, nondescript old flyrod, single action cheap reel, and home-tied flies.

When he met me after work, he brought his lunch with him. It consisted of a case of beer. "This," Dave said, "is also my boat cushion." I was impressed.

After a couple of hours on Clear Lake in the Bald Hills, Dave was the one who was impressed. He was one of those guys who said, "You get what you pay for." My cheap outfit outdid him at least two to one, even with my relaxed approach to fishing. The one competitive thing I did was not to waste time.

Dave died of a heart attack. He had a spare tire and did not exercise much at all, but he was a great and pleasant companion.

✿ ✿ ✿ ✿

Once when I was 14 or 15, I found myself in my rowboat well into the military end of the lake. A couple of young women in uniforms were not far away near some of the swimming lockers at the Soldiers' beach. I had always been able to whistle well and I was aware of the social practice of whistling at women known as the "wolf whistle." So I trilled away and the sound of girlish laughter resulted. A minute or two later there was an answering whistle, every bit as loud and beckoning as mine, followed by more laughter as a pair of young WAACs looked my way.

I knew how to whistle and that these older women were responding, but I couldn't for the life of me decide what I should do next. It was annoying and made me feel even more shy about females.

✿ ✿ ✿ ✿

Once Grandpa said to someone within my hearing range that an older woman who did some domestic work for the Gawleys had tidied up after one of her clients that morning and "that bed sure was one hell of a mess."

I repeated this remark to Larry Feir, only half understanding its significance, and, of course, Larry mentioned it to Grandpa. The old man gently informed me that I should be careful not to repeat that sort of information because "it would be bad for her reputation." This, of course, made me ask myself why Gramps had told anyone about the situation in the first place.

✿ ✿ ✿ ✿

It is remarkable that I do not ever recall fishing at American Lake with either Wayne Zimmerman or his son Steve. These two have been angling companions often, but always at other lakes, both alpine and lowland. More's the pity, because these two stalwarts meet all the qualifications – plus.

✿ ✿ ✿ ✿

It was many years before I learned to take the lake's temperature but I finally made that part of the ritual that I could zero in on to try to determine what made good conditions for fishing. Then I bought a fishing thermometer and put it on a cheap reel with monofilament line of medium weight. This became part of my tackle, and I wouldn't think of going out to fish without using it.

I recommend taking readings just under the surface and at 30 feet, where you will get most of your good fishing.

As the lake gets deeper from top to bottom, layers of water have about the same temperature pretty much around the lake. These layers are referred to by the experts as the thermocline, and they really play an important part in fish activity. When the temp is just right, fish get active and seem eager to bite.

Sometimes it is difficult to squeeze even one small fish out of my treasured American Lake. I can recall springs and early summers when you would swear the water was devoid of trout. At those times business was slow at the boathouse. These days came and went, and in the meantime Grandpa spent more time keeping warm and talking with all comers rather than renting out boats.

It never occurred to the old man, nor to me in my youthful bliss, that these dry spells were mainly caused by water temperature. Our state fisheries agents who know about all there is to know about kokanee and rainbows and cutthroats will tell you what optimum water temperatures are for the various species. I think I recall 55 degrees as just right for kokanee, but I also know from experience that water as warm as 70 degrees produced good results for me.

Of course, the depth at which one takes a temperature reading is key to understanding what is going on. You will find quite a variation from just under the surface and 30 or 50 feet down.

One year I recall a temp of 72 near the surface, and we were catching small perch with our trolling gear right out in the middle of the lake.

❂   ❂   ❂   ❂

Our privy was about half way up the hill that led down to the boathouse. It was tucked in next to the foundation of one of the houses on the property and not far from a magnificent Douglas fir tree. I do not recall a door on this facility but the "floorplan" was such that there was a sufficient sense of privacy.

The best thing about the privy was that it had a wonderful view of the lake through a large window without a pane. My own trips there were brief, but I was glad it was there when needed – window or no.

○ ○ ○ ○

My younger brother Paul Billy succeeded me for a year or two after I got old enough to get a summer job in the shipyards. But he never really warmed to fishing, despite the fact that the fish seemed to like him. When Uncle Oscar took us fishing for the first time in Steilacoom Lake, it was Paul who caught two fish while I got skunked and Uncle Oscar caught just one.

Paul often paid little attention to his rod. You would have to tell him he was getting a bite. Uncle Oscar teased him by calling him a "belly grabber," meaning he liked his sandwiches better than catching a fish.

○ ○ ○ ○

Perhaps I have given Grandpa a bit more credit as a chef than he was entitled to. But what he served up seemed to fill my needs, and I was used to eating a lot of good food at home. Paul, however, tells of one time when Grandpa was making pancakes and a single file of small ants was doing the lemming thing off his kitchen shelf. The tiny creatures plunged, one after another, into the pancake batter on the table below. Paul didn't say how heartily he ate on that occasion nor how the pancakes tasted. I guess Gramps could have used some reading glasses.

○ ○ ○ ○

Jim and I used to talk about schemes to catch more fish. One of these involved lowering a large net and baiting it so we could pull it up suddenly full of trout. We also thought it would be nice to devise a fishing machine that would hook the fish and play it before bringing it up to the surface. Ah, sportsmanship!

❂   ❂   ❂   ❂

The first time I saw a live catfish, I didn't know whether to laugh or be scared. I was fishing around the margin of our big dock and was right at a corner nearest the shore. It was a thrill to see a fish's tail poking out from under the dock, because I felt it must be a sizeable bass.

So I dropped my angleworm softly near the tail, which quickly turned around and became a face. It was an ugly face: wide mouth, myopic eyes, and barbels. These latter I had been warned about because they can inflict painful injury.

I caught the fish and presented it to Grandpa, being careful not to mess with its mouth and barbels.

So, when I rowed up toward the point with the military sign a few days later and explored a small lagoon in that area, I knew right away when I saw another catfish and another what they were.

This little lagoon was created by anchoring a log or two at the mouth of a small inlet. It served as a place for the folks who used the nearby cabins with the deaf Scottish caretaker. The vacationers probably swam there. Boats were tethered nearby.

It was a pretty little area with many water lilies and some other vegetation. The bottom of this small area was muddy – just what the catfish preferred. The catfish apparently came there to spawn and I must have just about wiped out the entire lake population of brown bullhead catfish that day, because I caught seven of the them, all from 13 to 17 inches long.

Grandpa was delighted. He had grown up in the Midwest and he was used to cooking and eating catfish. For my part, they were so ugly I didn't care to eat them. This was silly, of course, because fried catfish is a delicacy. But I sure had fun catching them for Grandpa.

❂   ❂   ❂   ❂

When we used to congregate in front of the boathouse, out over the springs, for our stillfishing each morning, there was an air of camaraderie among the regulars and politeness toward newcomers who were not rude themselves. Of course there was competition of a sort. Jim and I stood everyone on their heads for a while until they caught onto fishing with periwinkles.

Some fellows put great store in the feed they threw overboard to attract fish. Or at least they pretended to. I remember one fellow who put his feed – a mixture of oats and bran and salmon eggs and God knows what – into a detergent container. The laundry soap was called Duz and the box was a cheerful orange, white, and blue with big letters and a whirly design.

This guy had a good run of luck when he outfished all around him for awhile. Each time he hooked a fish and his rod bent nearly double, he let out a horselaugh and snorted, "Duz does it!" This was a motto the soap makers used and we all recognized. For a while he enjoyed his joke.

❂   ❂   ❂   ❂

It can be frightening when you ram the business end of a hook into your hand or some other part of your anatomy. The first time this happened to me, I thought I might get seriously sick.

But I enlisted the help of a nearby angler – we were at the access area and on dry land at the time – and things worked out okay. Fortunately, I always carry a small pair of side cutters as part of my fishing tackle. After I pushed the sharp end of the hook through the flesh of my finger and out, it was easy for the other guy to cut off the protruding end, and the hook came out easily.

So carry something you can cut off a hook with and don't panic. You will probably survive.

❁ ❁ ❁ ❁

I never got back to the skinny little cove over by where the old gray building stood. Many times I was in the area but was always intent on pursuing bass or trout to the exclusion of spending time on observing the carp.

The one time I was there as a fourteen-year-old, the cove was choked with really huge carp, apparently congregating for spawning purposes. Immediately I thought of my trusty yewwood bow that my Sunday School teacher had made and given to me as an attendance prize. Somewhere I had read of shooting carp with arrows and a line attached. Though this seemed like fun, I didn't know if it were legal and, besides, what the hell do you do with a ten pound carp?

❁ ❁ ❁ ❁

Speaking of carp, there was a wonderful cartoonist named Guindon who drew a one-panel cartoon centered around jokes relating to carp. A few people I worked with and I became fans and we were crushed when he took one of those leaves-of-absence from which many of our best cartoonists never return.

He had done a cartoon with part of a song about carp being sung by the lead character. So I wrote a pretty good little poem about carp and mailed it to him, care of the syndicate.

He replied, and I treasure his letter. He was gratified that I got into the spirit of his foolishness, which is about as good advice as anyone can ever give.

If it makes you laugh, it can't be all that bad.

❁ ❁ ❁ ❁

— A Lifelong Love —

I don't think I know anyone who has become married without feeling that their marital state would remain solid for life. But the length of my relationship with American Lake has surpassed two marriages and has whittled into a third.

And, like many marriages, I got into the situation with the lake almost by accident. I was born just two years before the Great Depression began and was enjoying my second year at J.P. Stewart Intermediate School in Tacoma when fate beckoned and my employment at the lake suddenly became reality. When Grandpa made his offer of "forty dollars a month and room and board," there was no way of knowing I was taking up a lifelong contract.

During my checkered career, mainly as writer, editor, and teacher, there have been opportunities to move to other areas: Boise, Idaho; and Shelton, Washington being two. The only time I succumbed to a "better offer," it was to move near San Francisco to teach high school journalism for maybe $300 a year more than I was making. But living in Eastbay was not to my liking. For one thing, I never even unpacked my tackle after I looked into the fishing situation. So I have never caught a striped bass, more's the pity.

Immovable Me

Please do not hold me to precise dates when they do not matter. I am over 90 now and still have most of my marbles, but am disinclined to research stuff that isn't important. Anyway, I do not remember for sure fishing in American Lake the year we moved to California and just as rapidly moved back. Our move was in August, however, and it is likely I fished a number of times before that month. And we were back the following June, so it is not likely I stayed away from my favorite haunt the rest of that year.

Until I had to give up my boat and trailer and all that went with them in 2005, I fished frequently at American.

You Can Look It up

From the early days, I kept records of my fishing dates. In fact, I used to keep track of my golf scores, my tennis matches, even results of touch football games. Most of these were just numbers to mull in idle hours, but I liked to think the fishing stats were of some use.

For example, the question always arose: Where can I get to a spot to catch some fish, preferably trout? A quick perusal of records shows that at this time last year and the year before, I was doing well at such and such a lake at such and such a time of the day while using this or that bait or lure in a particular location.

Get the picture? Well, the records did help to some extent, and I was glad to have them to fall back on. They told part of the story of my life. For example they say that the last year I had my boat and trailer, I went fishing 47 times. A good portion of that would have been at American Lake. If I cared, I could look it up, but it is academic now, which means you don't care either.

Most years, that number of fishing trips was probably typical, but the number of trips is not really important. What is important is something I could not measure, and that is: to what extent did I enjoy the outing?

No Cuts, No Brookies

When I first started to keep fishing records, they read something like a boxscore, which is not surprising since I loved baseball almost as much as fishing. Each trip took a line all the way across the page. It had columns of varying widths for lake name, time fished, weather, and a skinny column for every kind of fish I could think of. So I would wind up with 0 cutthroat, 3 rainbows, 0 brook trout, 0 Dolly Varden, etc. I can't remember if

I kept track of spiny rays – I doubt it and could look it up but am too tired.

These early records proved too cumbersome. I got tired writing in all the zeros. And I kept discovering kinds of fish I never knew existed, which complicated things. So I went to a diary form. This was more flexible and I could make observations about birds and animals and anything I wanted.

In early spring I would pull out the records and try to figure where to go to catch a fish. This worked out okay. Basically, I learned that it was a good thing not to get excited about trout fishing in American Lake until about May 1. The water was too cold most years until then. I also learned that I most often found fish trolling in later years at about 30 feet down or on the surface.

So I would encourage any persistent fisherman to keep some kind of records. You might get some use out of them. And include water temperature with your observations.

There Were Others

When we were kids just starting to fish, it was almost unthinkable to consider fishing in any lake but American unless someone gave me or my friends an unexpected lift to another place. Oh, you could take the Spanaway bus and ride to the end of the line, then hike the rest of the way to the park and rent a boat if you had the lucre. But you weren't going to get the same value as by getting on the Lake Shore Stage Lines bus to American Lake.

In my junior year in high school, I was invited on a hiking and camping trip to an alpine lake south and east of Tacoma with three high school friends. I fell in love with fly fishing in pristine waters. We stuck it out for a number of days with primitive equipment and lack of experience. This opened up new vistas to me and I spent many happy hours and days fishing in mountain lakes.

There are many lowland lakes to fish in Pierce and neighboring counties, particularly Thurston County. I fished in a number of them many times over the years.

What, Me Pay?

Of course, I got spoiled with free boat rental for some years as a perk of my employment and, I guess, a kind of retirement bonus from Grandpa. It has always gone against the grain with me to pay to rent a boat. Grandpa remained in his employment at the boathouse for a few years after Paul and I worked for him. He was eventually booted out and a guy named Bert Thomas, a long-distance swimmer of some note, ran the boathouse for a while. Sometime later a nice man named Anderson took over and provided service for years until his death. His family still runs the boathouse.

But the boat rental business is barely alive today. Firch's has long since folded. There was a boat rental business for years on the western shore near the seaplane base. I kept my homemade boat there for a year or two when I was a young teacher, and I fished almost every summer morning before breakfast. When I came home to my place in Lakewood, I usually had fish.

As near as I can figure it without going into convulsions, I fished for 63 years in American Lake. There were times when "class failures" and getting skunked multiple times in a row made me take a holiday from the lake, but I always came back.

In later years I was in touch with my friend Jim Hutson. I played slow pitch baseball for his team and we had lunch together a time or two. Jim said he never fished in American anymore, even though his office was in Tillicum. He was busy with baseball, football, and basketball, as both player and coach.

Old Friends Are Best

But I stuck with American even through lean years when, as one super friendly black man I encountered near the boathouse said, all he had seen caught that year were "ring-tailed perch." I am still thinking about that one.

As near as I can figure, I started fishing in American Lake in 1942 and fished there at least once every year through 2005. Some of my friends have been married nearly that long – and to one person. But I got along with the lake better than any woman I ever knew, even though I felt it was trying to drown me a time or two.

After all these years, American Lake is still the lake of my dreams. If it were any better, it would be too perfect.

What a break to have such an experience during my formative years. Those days on our big raft of a dock must surely have rivaled those of Mark Twain's characters on the Mississippi.

I still dream from time to time of fishing with Jim or alone. The lake is American and I know they're in there. I am always hoping to feel once more that pulsing on my rod that pleases so much. You might even say I got a few.

Homer Post editing copy at age 85 for the local newspaper in Tacoma. He was working part time when this picture was taken.

Special Thanks to:

Weston Davis

Chelsea Davis

Carol Raphael

Dave Raphael

www.ingramcontent.com/pod-product-compliance
Lightning Source LLC
Chambersburg PA
CBHW020002290326
41935CB00007B/269